LIGHTBULB MOMENTS
MIRACLES UPON AWAKENING

DOUG McPHILLIPS

Also, by Doug McPhillips:
Other Visionary Stories:
NOVELS:
From Darkness to Light.
Awake to my Gutted Dream.
The Sword of Discernment.
Santiago Traveller.
I, Prophet.
Master's at my table.
The Guru of Jerusalem.
We are upside down. (Biography)
The Wicklow Way.
The Adventures of Ace McDice.
Instant Karma & Grace.
The Credo.
Reflections of an Old Man.
Reincarnation of the Assassin
Masters of Introspection.
Journey to a hermit's haven.
The Rise and Rise of a 4th Reich
Grandad's tales are tall and true.
Into Action: Alcoholics for Jesus.
A Camino Guide Book.
Country Camino. (Album).
Santiago Traveller. (Album).
Soul Fact. (Album).

Apart from any fair dealing for private study, research, criticism or review, as permitted under the Copyright Act, no part may be reproduced by any process without the editor's written permission.
Doug McPhillips Circa 2025
ISBN. Paperback 978-1-7638868-3-4 eBook 978-1-7638868-4-1

National Library of Australia Catalogue-in-Publication data: New Holy Bible, International Version, Hodder & Stoughton, 1980.

Alcoholics Anonymous, 4th Edition, AA World Service, 1976.

As Bill sees it, 8th Print, AA World Service, 2017

Daily Reflections, 11th Print, AA World Service, 2014.

Journey to the Inner Mountain, Hodder & Stoughton, James Cowan, 2002.

The Choice is always ours, Jove Publishing, 1997.

Santiago traveller, Ingram Spark, Doug McPhillips, 2018.

The Meaning of Myth as a guide to life, Simon & Schuster, 1999.

Google research- Authors Unknown.

This book blends fact and fiction. All characters in this novel are factual or fictional, and the names of people living at the time may be real or imagined. Any resemblance to actual events, locales, or persons, living or dead, is purely coincidental; however, what is applicable is real. Where poetic license transforms fact into fiction, names have been altered to protect the innocent.

For all souls working with their Higher Self

And for those seeking acceptance.

Content.

Introduction. 7

Chapter 1. The Alpha. 11

Chapter 2. Wild Ways on My Way. 23

Chapter 3. Awesome Eagles. 33

Chapter 4. Acceptance. 41

Chapter 5. Symbols and Signs of The Way. 49

Chapter 6. The Spiritual Quest. 59

Chapter 7. Enlightenment. 71

Chapter 8. More Mythical Stories. 81

Chapter 9. The Last Hurrah. 93

Chapter 10. Epilogue. 101

Introduction

Looking back in contemplation on my life from birth until my now newly awakened dotage, I am mindful of the events that have triggered moments of inspiration, prompted changes, creative output, and sometimes inspired transformative insights that led me unwittingly down a new pathway. Sometimes, either out of fear, I took the safe way, or bravery stepped out upon the road less travelled, all of which I recall with deep feelings for what came to pass, and in which I now choose to relate to you herein, for our mutual benefit. For you, it may prove to be insightful, and for me, a cathartic attempt to come to terms with my understanding and acceptance of what has transpired, as well as what I call 'Lightbulb Moments'—miracles that occur upon awakening, along the way.

The content herein is influenced by the times the events took place, the boundaries of my psychological state, and the analytical mindsets that existed then, as well as the indoctrinations of Christian theology, historical antecedents, and the progression of time to a modest viewpoints of nature, spiritual intuition and the hardcore lessons of life's experiences as they relate to what took place and the lessons learnt therein.

Through it all, much of what transpired occurred at times of great personal suffering, after which enlightenment emerged, ultimately leading to my understanding and well-being. In particular, creative output came upon me after periods of intense despair, a sense of being alone in the world or at the point of tragic circumstance. My wounds were a source of healing through an outpouring of the heart, expressed in poetry, songs, and oral storytelling. The springs of emotional pull came at a price, a particular spiritual discipline that gave meaning and purpose to my life at that time.

As for the times that existed throughout the various intervals of my life, each decade brought with it changes that advanced from my distinctive Orthodox Christian spirituality, focused on the sufferings of Jesus to save humanity, to new age philosophies, a breakdown of old ideas that no longer seemed to work for me, to parallel philosophies, like that of Jung's approach to the wounded spirit destined to be heal by a spiritualist viewpoint in contracts to the traditional lessons of both the Old and New Testaments.

Like many for a time, I initially embraced the New Age alternative view of a loving God, with the naivety of a starry-eyed optimist, confident that with a futurist focus, success in a spiritual sense would ultimately unfold. That it was God's mistake and not man's folly, that the orthodoxy of Christ Church got it all wrong, and that man mistakenly embraced the material world of the devil, who created a lesser divinity. It was right if one wanted to get ahead in the world. However, over time, I learnt that the secret to a spiritual life is to learn to live in this world but not be of it. That is to live within the spirit of what one may perceive as a God of one's understanding and be guided with faith in handing over to the spiritual essence for guidance.

Such New Age beliefs are widespread in culture and the imagination, but have little fundamental evidence to support their long-term benefits to one's spiritual well-being or their contribution to humanity's spiritual progress for the good of all concerned. Hollywood has popularised Gnosticism, a New Age view of a lesser divinity that runs the show, as seen in films like The Matrix, the documentary on the Gospel of Judas, and successful books that appeal to a broad audience, such as Dan Brown's The Da Vinci Code, which claims a historical reliability on what is in truth pure speculation. These New Age views offer a blind promise of privileged insight and elite knowledge, but one must be aware of the dangers in embracing them.

The dangers of embracing the New Age religions of the heart have challenged the enlightenment claims that science and rational analytical investigation pave the road to truth, and that the human mind can encompass all reality. The poets and writers of the English Romantic times contended that our inner experiences of emotions and intuition also opened us to a world of truth, which science and rational enquiry hold no relevance or authority. To escape the arid landscape of postmodern materialism and make life bearable, many today, like the romantics of the eighteenth century, who faced the stark materialism of the world, seek refuge in rational spirituality, which has given rise to a New Age movement.

Whilst one might waltz down the aisles of lightweight authors' modern spirit ideas, living under the safe umbrella of a New Age coexistence with the less comfortable older traditional form of spirituality, it is not hard to realise that every age of influence exists, which may well take one away from the logical linear doctrines of faith and morals that have stood the test of time. It is not to say that the New Age phenomenon is not worthy of consideration. In truth, I hasten to add that in my experience, whilst alternate philosophies of belief served me for a time and influenced my creativity, in the main over decades, they are (were) just a whiff of smoke along the road towards the destiny that the real maker of all, who remains a mystery to humanity, has us walk.

Just as New Age reality can be complex to fathom and fully understand, the many religions of the world themselves are sometimes outside the boundaries of fundamental convictions that dismiss conventional religions' teachings with answers that have yet to be proven in the long term. The New Age doctrines, on some level, are not absolute truths, but rather somewhat subjective views that might best be described as narcissistic ideals, perceived as such. It is the creation of one's reality, which the brain perceives, through the influence of the creative imagination, something experienced through the senses as good, bad, or indifferent, that one responds to as reality. The mind is tricked into believing that one is all, that one invents one's existence, and that we are our universe. Like we have created God instead of God creating Man. Such a claim has no objective truth, which is pure nonsense.

One may hold traditional orthodox beliefs in the structure of one's soul search, yet at the same time, unwittingly, in an emotional sense, find profound spiritual significance in Nature and the species of the earth, and believe in the interconnection of all life as expressed in branches of related organisms in the physical surrounds. Whilst one's views may be expressed through creative outpouring, one must not lose sight of the fact that there is an equality between the logical, linear half of the brain and the innovative, intelligent side of the other.

The dialogue above serves as an informative guide to this author's lifetime of experience across various doctrines of faith and morals, as well as life experiences, suffering, the darkest moments of the soul, and moments of miraculous insight. What follows are brief extracts of those lightbulb moments of great inspiration and expectation that have occurred for this author. This book serves as a catalytic doctrine of recall for all who seek insight into the soul's journey, particularly my own.

CHAPTER 1.

THE ALPHA

In Christian doctrine, the symbol for Alpha from the Greek alphabet denotes the beginning. Whilst it represents a biblical reference to the beginning of time, it is also relevant to the beginning of this author's life, which parallels that of many a man born of a woman on this earth at that time.

It was no small historical coincidence that I was born of Irish parents in 1944. A momentous event happened that year- D Day, which precipitated the end of the war in Europe and the subsequent defeat of Japan in 1945. It also heralded the onset of the Atomic Age after the decimation of Hiroshima and Nagasaki. I knew nothing of this at the time as I was to busy sucking on a surrogate mothers boobs. I have been doing that for most of my life.

As the Allies opened the gates of the German concentration camps to reveal the horrors of the Holocaust, the devastation of the aftermath of another world war, and the impact of economic injustices that befell the world at large at the time, I was getting accustomed to life with my parents who had been married for only one year when I was born. Flashbacks of those early days in the cot in the small two-bedroom flat above the Read and Fotheringham Produce store. Memories flood back of Dad chasing a rat from the store below my bedroom. The sound of his footsteps on the wooden stairs as he arrived home from work at the end of the day made my heart race. The playpen on the verandah was where I was often left for hours on my own during the day, while Mum busied herself in the kitchen preparing the evening meal. She seemed to slip into postnatal depression almost immediately after I was born, as simultaneously her milk dried up, and a surrogate mother took over the duties of filling my thirst for nourishment. It was not just the food I needed, but affection as well. I seem to have known even as a baby that I was abandoned. Unlike many mums who suffered postnatal depression, hers never really left her. Medical science didn't know much about bipolar disorder back then, and her mood took those extremes of highs and lows all too often during my formative years. From her later behaviour, I now know she loved me very much, but didn't know how to show it. It left me craving affection, which later led me down a path of trouble and strife, which I've long since recovered from. The feelings of childhood abandonment led me to display early signs of codependence and a need to be a people pleaser. My mother's inferiority complex didn't help it, and her only claim to fame, being me, was to get any attention by encouraging me to perform in front of an audience. I mistakenly took this as the way to be loved. It took me until adulthood to realise the way out was an inward journey, but for a time, my feelings manifested into depression and anxiety.

My father was often absent, building an empire that would become an engineering masterpiece of its time. He preferred to be at work rather than at home with domestic responsibilities. He was a man of action, prioritising service to others over his family. However, he was a good provider, and soon enough, we moved to a larger home, which was a place of great experiences for me, but also one of much sadness.

The house's backyard was a mix of artificial features and nature's way; it included a shed for storing firewood, a woodpile where Dad cut the timber for the fuel stove, a chip heater supply line for bathing, and fuel for the copper for washing clothes, a tank to store water pumped from an underground bore, a chicken coop for our egg supply, and a block to chop the heads of a couple of chooks for Sunday lunch. The backyard was outside the Garden of Eden, adjacent to Casey's orchard, which was blocked by an extensive tuck-and-groove fence. My entrance into the realm of God's creation came after I was tempted to eat of the tree of knowledge, an orange tree with fruit hanging over our side of the fence. Mum caught me at the back of the shed eating a ' stolen ' orange that I had picked from the neighbour's tree. So there I was, no more than four years of age, being marched off to face Mr. Casey and tell him that I had committed a sin and stolen an orange. I arrived at his door with fear and trembling, expecting the worst punishment that only God could dish out. To my surprise, he forgave me without penance and showed me around his orchard full of plum trees, oranges, apples, and mandarins.

Furthermore, he invited me to come around anytime and help myself to fresh fruit whenever I desired. It was then that I never needed to steal anything again. The lesson I learnt was as in the Bible: "Ask and you shall receive!

About this time, I befriended the neighbour's grandson on the other side of the Garden of Eden. We were small boys, but our parents didn't mind if we vanished into the nearby bushland for the day, chasing rabbits and lizards and being cautious of snakes whenever they were spotted. Looking back, I realise that our parents were irresponsible. We later engaged in many outdoor activities without our parents' watchful eyes, becoming proficient in climbing trees to collect bird eggs, taking a family shotgun to go duck shooting without permission, and being forgiven for bringing home a dead duck full of shotgun pellets. Of course, we were a bit older — about ten years — by the time we could prove our skill at fishing and duck shooting as mature hunters.

Fate had it that my uncle John, my mother's younger brother, who was only twelve, came to live with us. He suffered from rheumatic fever, which caused severe illness in his heart and joints. John, the youngest of thirteen siblings, was in my mother's care for the next two years of his life. Mum devoted herself to his every need, and I didn't mind, as I was just three when he arrived, and he helped fill my days with activity and interest. When not bedridden, he would organise fights for local kids, teach them and me how to box, go horse riding, ride wild bulls at local rodeos, or entertain many high school girls who were fascinated by his loving personality and good looks. Mum carried the burden of attending to John with complete devotion. I didn't mind, just as long as I had John as my older guide. Then one fateful day, it happened: John died unexpectedly. His heart gave out, and mine felt broken, it seemed forever.

In a spirit of recovery, I stayed with my Uncle Fred for a while. I was a small boy of nearly five, in the company of a middle-aged bushman high in the mountain ranges near the small town of Nymboida, Gumbaynggirr Country. Nymboida is the first township along the Clarence River, and the river is home to the longest whitewater trail in Australia. It was a cool place to be as I learnt to spot a platypus, fish for trout, and shoot my first bird with a .303 army rifle. These days, the mountain countryside is a National Park teeming with wildlife of every species. It was the same back then, but wilder.

My uncle worked as a tree feller, and we would take off for a week or two, living in a tent high up in the mountains. During the day, I sat on his knee as he drove a bulldozer, selected a tree to push over, and spent the day with an axe, cutting off the limbs and using a chain to drag it to a bush trail to add to the pile already prepared for the next log truck to transport to the nearest timber mill, destined for use in building houses in the growing township along the North Coast in the 1950s. We lived on fresh fish caught from the river and the occasional rabbit shot by my uncle, a crack marksman who later became the New South Wales small-bore rifle champion. We ate beside a log fire in the evening and watched as the dingos' eyes flashed from the firelight, coming in close and howling for some leftover food. It was when Uncle Fred grew tired of the danger they posed that he fired a warning shot over their heads to scare them away. He could just as easily have killed the pack's leader, but that wasn't his way. I was never afraid when curled under the blanket in his tent, knowing I was safe as long as that fire stayed well stoked and burned until dawn. It became a natural occurrence to fall asleep listening to the howls of the dingos in the nearby hills, with my uncle lying nearby, a rifle at his side.

Those were the days of my imagination and a reality that was more than most children could ever experience. I returned home to my parents, where I helped local flood victims. Our little place of abode soon filled with people of every nationality, with whom I had to share the bedroom floor and line up for the bathroom and outside toilet. No sooner had it become somewhat unbearable than the floodwaters subsided, and everyone set forth to clean up the silt and mud that remained after nature had wreaked its damage once again. While the house was quiet again, I had little time to feel lonely, for Dad had us move into a new home he built, and I was off to school.

The beginning of my schooling started with a taunt from my Uncle Heppy: " He's off to school, we Dougie, with his bag upon his shoulder…" were the last words I heard from his lips as I walked out the door into a new and broader world. I loved my Uncle Heppy, but he could be cruel when it suited him. He was to stay for another week of his holiday. So, despite the tears in my eyes, I stoically gave my Mum and Dad a wave, smiled through clenched teeth at my uncle, and took to the pathway for a new education.

The memory of early schooling comes in flashes now. I remember meeting new friends and being reacquainted with those I had known through family connections since birth. It was a school for a few children, and the 'Sisters of No Mercy' were but two or three nuns who shared the education duties in two class lots. Junior primary was from kindergarten to year six, all housed in one room with three rows of desks. So the youngest, like me, were being taught the rudiments of reading, writing, and arithmetic on one side of the room, while the teacher skipped across a row to teach another subject to the middle row. Then, those in the far row, who were more advanced, were taught subjects in readiness for high school the following year. The high school layout in the next room was the same: the first row consisted of first-year high school students, the second row consisted of second-year high school students, and the last row consisted of intermediate school students. Looking back now, I realise how difficult it must have been for those three teachers juggling classes from kindergarten to high school. We took frequent canings and smacks from those holy women who did their very best in a co-ed school of (perhaps) some 150 students in all. They did their best to drum the rudiments of Latin, French, and mathematics from the earliest days into our thick heads. Religious studies, of course, were a must, and attendance at Holy Mass before school became a part of their daily discipline, as did the regular duties of us boys to clean the school toilets once a week. A tough job for any kid starting from the age of reason and wondering, with some fear and trepidation, where it might all lead.

Whilst struggling with the French lingo, Latin came easier; it had to, for the local one-eyed Irish priest selected six of us boys, as young as seven at the time, to serve as altar boys. He had us sit on a long stool and cracked a long stock whip over our heads if we became lost in translation with the Latin words. Even today, a Latin phrase may burst forth when I hear a loud noise or a car backfire. I was not destined to graduate from that school, for at the end of year seven, my Dad, in his wisdom, sent me off to boarding school in Sydney. The event that precipitated this decision was the drowning of my best mate, whom I had known since birth. I had witnessed my Uncle John's death before I was five years old. So there I was at age twelve, having seen the drowning of my best mate and unable to do anything about it except fall into a sad and deep melancholy. I would miss the wild days in the bushland, leaving a lot of stuff in the handlebars of girls' bikes, the occasional kiss behind an old oak tree, and cuddling high up on a pile of flour bags in the bakehouse of a favourite girl. More than anything else, it was the rough and tumble of playing rugby league in the north coast competitions that I would miss most. I also came to miss playing chicken, like James Dean of movie fame in "Rebel Without a Cause," on my bicycle, which I later emulated by driving my car soon after being issued a driving licence.

As a side note, some heads were not as thick as others who attended that school. Graduates include Steve Moneghetti, a renowned Australian long-distance runner, and Thomas Keneally, a celebrated author and recipient of the Australian National Living Treasure award. Additionally, Rob Shehadie, an actor known for shows like "Pizza" and "Housos," and Peter Skrzynecki, a poet and writer, are also part of this distinguished group. Notable alums. More recently, Philip Hughes, the cricketer who tragically died in a Sheffield cricket match in 2014, was remembered as a graduate of the school as well as the local High School.

So I attended a renowned GPS rugby school, St. Joseph's College. I had been reasonably tall until twelve, but didn't grow much afterwards. Consequently, I never achieved higher grades in Rugby Union at school, settling for playing at the C or D level. Given that the teams were ranked down to twelve, I was playing at a level best suited to my strengths at the time. The school taught a greater variety of subjects than my old alma mater, including modern and ancient history, geography, wool classing, singing, dancing, and music. School cadets were a must to be involved in, and while I didn't relish the idea of training for war, I nevertheless fell in line with it, although I was often on detention parade for misbehaviour.

I was destined to become a coxswain in the school rowing squad. I excelled at guiding boys much older than me in rowing, fitness sessions, and distance running, and I ultimately earned an honour blazer for my efforts. Like the nuns, the Marist Brothers knew how to dish out some painful canings, and too many of those I prefer to bury in the memory bank forever.

Schoolboy pranks were the norm for us country kids, but my best claim to fame was being a " North Coaster. " A number of us travelled to and from school at the beginning and end of each term on the North Coast mail. We rode in second-class carriages, which were divided into opposing bench seats made of railway-green tanned leather, wide enough to hold four boys' bums with room to spare for spreading out. Above each seat was a wire rack for luggage, and on the dark wooden walls hung photos of bush scenes depicting railway activity or the unveiling of a new train. Each compartment had a metal foot warmer, which was particularly useful in winter when the floor was cold to the touch. Placing one's socked feet on the gas-filled cylinder guaranteed warmth and helped with the residue of chilblains in the not-too-distant future. We also had a large water container and a drinking glass on a shelf attached to the wall. I don't recall any of us ever drinking that water; we preferred to buy a tea bag with hot water in a polystyrene cup and railway biscuits at station stops along the way. The train stopped at major country stations for ten minutes, giving enough time to stretch out legs, visit the toilet, and breathe some fresh air away from the soot spewing that entered the carriages from the coal-fired engines that pulled the train to the next destination.

Heading home on that train was always an adventure. We didn't sleep much, so we closed the sliding carriage doors, binding the handles with our school ties to avoid being disturbed by the night guard. Once he collected our tickets, we were left to our own devices. We amused ourselves by smoking a few "rolled my own" cigarettes and drinking Horehound beer, a non-alcoholic beverage made from double hops and sugar cane. It was not long after those early teens that I graduated to full-strength alcohol, much to my initial delight and later peril, for I was a die-hard alcoholic from the first drink and found myself on the road to prediction- at least that is what I had condemned myself to believe for many years before I begin to wise up.

The train snaked its way north, and soon enough, we lost most of Joey's rabble between Newcastle and Foster, and many at Taree. Most of our trip was spent singing songs or counting the different types of timber that made up the telegraph poles along the route.

The idea was to select a tree type and determine how many telegraph poles were made from it over a specified distance. Along the side of the track, each pole had an identification mark. This identification helped in several ways: it allowed utilities to track the source and species of the wood, understand its strength and durability, and ensure proper maintenance and replacement strategies. Like TT for tallow wood, PP for Pine, or GG for Grey Gum. Whoever picked the most of a species over a given number of rounds won the right to another beer or to punch out an opponent without any payback retaliation. On one trip north, Chris from Kranbach, another intrepid traveller, got the bright idea to grab the water bottle and was about to pour a glass of water for a fellow passenger. Instead, as quick as a flash, he threw the bottle out the window.

As luck would have it, the train passed a railway siding, and the bottle suddenly shattered over the concrete platform. The guard in the next carriage happened to be leaning out the window at the time and caught the action. Chris grabbed his suitcase and quickly made a getaway into the next carriage with the train guard in hot pursuit. Chris was due to alight at the next station, so before the guard could grab him, he opened the carriage door and jumped from the moving train. The last thing we witnessed was Chris's suitcase case bursting open with his worldly possessions flying in all directions, and the escaping youth rolling over and over along the platform. That was the last time we saw Chris; he never returned to school. I wonder what happened to him now. He was always in strife over some mischief or another. So I trust his life improved through the gaining of wisdom.

In my early school years, the schoolboy heroes and classmates seemed to live along that coastline. It was not uncommon for the classmate football heroes to appear in the local newspaper articles during the holidays. I, too, had fifteen minutes of fame when Dad announced to the local journalist that I had won an honour blazer for rowing. Before long, I had fifteen minutes of fame with a photo of the winning crew, with me as Coxswain, appearing in the press. Outside of bushfires, floods, and the devastation of drought, news to report was scarce for country journalists, apart from human interest stories, the annual agricultural show, radio events, and athletic contests.

The holidays were a time to catch up with some primary school buddies, but in time, I soon found we had little in common in my teens. I used to amuse myself with long walks along the beach or some other lone activity, for I always thought I was destined for something different, but it never seemed to eventuate. When it did, it was wine, women and song that fueled the lonesome hero, and living dangerously behind the wheel. It was by luck or God's good grace that I survived to manhood.

When I returned to school, I always caught the evening train with a mate from near Coffs Harbour. We devised a plan to make life easier for the three months of each term. Our long journey back involved discussing what we had done during the holidays. Like all North Coast boys, we were a very close group and protected each other's best interests. David and I arrived at Central Station early on the first day of term. We would check the list for our allotted dormitory and help each other set up. Firstly, finding the best sprung bed and the most comfortable horsehair mattress. Then we would move it near a window with a view towards the city for the best vista. Once we unpacked our clothing into a locker, we headed to town for breakfast and spent the day watching the latest movies and twenty-four-hour newsreels before catching the bus back to school, leaving us with a roaring headache after too much screen time. We kept up this ritual for the five years we attended that school.

Joeys held the place of pride in the GPS, among the great public schools of Sydney. It was not so much for educational ability or thought; the record shows many fine academic graduates. It was, and still is, the best of graduates in the sporting arena, producing more international stars in Rugby, cricket, and athletics than the rest combined historically.

CHAPTER 2.

WILD WAYS ON MY WAY.

It could also be suggested that we had the greatest wild men and rogues during my time at school. In time, they too learnt to take the rough with the smooth, as we all had to do, or face the consequences of corporal punishment—an ever-frequent occurrence for those who stepped beyond the rules, treading our path at their peril.

Some events transpired that, to this day, cause me grief when recalled, while others bring a smile to my face. The memory of the hatred between O'Farrell and Morocco as they slugged it out punch for punch during a lunchtime brawl lingers. The Marist brother who officiated the dinner watched until the two bloodied enemies stood exhausted. He then asked casually, "Are you finished?" He then proceeded to crack their heads together to end the fight. On another occasion, a more serious incident occurred when two senior boys, Lynch and Holden, took the College speedboat out on the harbour at night, returning to school at dawn after a night out. They were greeted by Brother 'B J', who produced a bamboo cane as they came out of the showers. We all stood like naked statues while we watched those boys being canned to within an inch of their lives.

My mischief-making involved raiding Carrot Canyon, the food storage area, and the kitchen for more food for me and my mates; blocking all the outlets to the showers and causing a flood; walking across the wall of a full-flowing dam and getting washed downstream; and throwing a toilet roll out of a train window, hitting the Master of Discipline fair square in the face as he poked his head out. I recall many incidents where I faced severe punishment while others escaped without consequences. To the best of my recollection, everything balances out evenly. Although all these events occurred during my time as a student, I must add that the Marist Brothers' education served as a "great lever" for students regardless of our station in life. Joeys encouraged high performance in every endeavour, and they're effective for a misspent youth—a transformative educational institution. In essence, it's a school that significantly impacts students' academic performance, enabling them to achieve greater outcomes and approach life with the will to win, regardless of its obstacles.

Those were the early days after leaving school, which proved to be a time of more devilment than one might expect from a young elite man of private school education living in a conservative community in the early 1960s.

In 1960s Australia, the dominant value system was characterised by a strong sense of national pride, optimism about the future, and a gradual shift towards social change while questioning traditional norms. Although there was still a solid emphasis on family values and community, the decade also witnessed the rise of youth culture, challenges to established authority, and an increasing focus on individual rights and social equality. Key factors include the impact of the Cold War, the Vietnam War, the civil rights movement, and the emergence of rock and roll music. This era marked a departure from conservative values and a push for greater social justice, equality, and individual freedom.

Youth culture was about to explode even before "teenager" became synonymous with trouble and strife. We were locked into conservatism in jobs, family values, religious practices, and the laws of the land, but in reality, we rallied against all of this in the face of explosive change.

A new dawn emerged in the mid-1950s, marked by Elvis Presley's image of a clean-cut counterculture, which stemmed from his music's fusion of black and white genres and his bold, energetic performances. These performances began to challenge the conservative norms of the time. This rebellious attitude, particularly his suggestive dancing, sparked both controversy and fascination among us youth. He became a symbol of youth rebellion and a cultural icon, influencing fashion, music, and youth culture. My hero, James Dean, had not yet emerged for me when Elvis came along with songs and a series of movies that showcased his themes and style. I, like my rebellious mates, copied his look with a kiss curl in our greasy back hairstyles, lacquered with California Poppy oil, tucked-in shirts with turned-up collars, half-rolled sleeves, black, pinked, flecked stovepipe jeans, and blue suede shoes. We aimed to impress not just our peers but any girl who caught our fancy and who also embraced the culture of dressing in the fashions of the day, listening to Elvis's rock n' roll, watching his hip movements at the movies, and emulating the girls who surrounded him.

As a confused youth caught between the conservatism of my parents' era and the freedom of a new age, I suffered like many of my peers after leaving school. I was moody, often isolated, and engaged in risky pursuits. Before Bob Dylan came along and announced, "The Times They Are A-Changin," they truly were. Meanwhile, there were counterculture icons we imitated, as they seemed to articulate, in both word and deed, what we were grappling with at the time.

When James Dean emerged, the term 'teenager' was relatively new, but youth culture was ready to explode, bringing significant changes in attitudes towards music, style, conformity, and sexuality. In Life, Dean visits a group of students from his old high school. Those young students likely saw Dean in Rebel Without a Cause and went on to help usher in the massive social changes that occurred during the 1960s counterculture movement, the effects of which are still felt today.

I had been a teenage idol of Jimmy Dean since my days of playing chicken on push bikes, emulating the thrill of crash or burn, ever since I first watched James Dean in "Rebel Without a Cause," then "East of Eden," and "Giant." This fascination with a hero who defied social norms inspired me, in later years, to write and record a song titled "The Loner, James Dean," which can still be heard on Spotify or any other music platform. Dean's sullen moods and mumbling diction influenced those of us who felt we didn't fit the system we graduated through in the late 1950s and early 1960s. It also affected fellow actors Marlon Brando and Montgomery Clift, along with rising star Anthony Perkins, after his tragic death.

We youths of the Saturday afternoon movies took to heart the style and living objectives they advocated more seriously than the Sunday morning preaching of our local priest and the do-good attitude of the congregation's holier-than-thou approach to community living. James Dean was renowned for his relaxed and laid-back style. His typical choice of a simple white t-shirt, blue jeans, an occasional leather jacket, and sunglasses exemplified this. For the most part, classic essentials were Dean's go-to. So, we soon graduated from Elvis-style to more traditional Dean dress, including the famous high cuffs on our Jeans, but I never gave up on blue suede shoes.

I did my best to fit into social norms, but now and then, I would break free, drive recklessly, play chicken, get hopelessly drunk, or get involved with a girl of ill repute, much to my parents' disgust. I was more than happy to move on from the shackles of living under my parents' roof when I was transferred to another town as a banker. I soon left the rigid banking career and joined public service for a few years. During this time, I began to smoke and drink more heavily, frequent bars, and mix with journalists, writers, and leftists who had moved beyond the maddening crowd of materialists to a more anti-establishment lifestyle. It was a form of protest against traditional values, but it never truly gained traction. The theme rejected conformity and consumerism in mainstream culture, expressed through various art forms, including literature, poetry, music, and painting. I was on the fringe of this but soon moved on, being more interested in drinking and having a good time with the opposite sex than in trying to align myself with another movement. By then, I was also into writing poetry, listening to folk music, and reading the works of Hemingway, Hess, and other notables. I no longer felt the need to prove myself to the pseudo-intellectuals.

I had more freedom in public service than I ever did in my banking career, but I pushed the boundaries to a great degree. My usual parking spot in the city was in the police car park. As my car was white, like the cop cars, I took it upon myself to gain access to free parking for a whole year until I was pulled over by a policeman and chastised for parking there illegally. I professed my innocence and swore I would never do it again. I noted afterwards that the police had installed a boom gate and a guard at the entrance. Not only did I secure employment as a tradesperson to install the gate, but I also created a full-time guard position. I felt justified in what I had achieved in this regard.

My three-and-a-half-year stint as a public service employee enhanced my opportunities to live a life of carefree danger and not-so-wise responsibility. I was tasked with signing off on jobs ranging from providing coaxial cable down the main street of Sydney's CBD to conducting area strength measurements for television. The first example ultimately delayed the recent installation of light rail along George Street. Although cable installation began in the 1960s, the paperwork for these jobs was stored in the archives of the General Post Office (GPO). Consequently, when the street was dug up, construction work on the rail line hit many live cables, resulting in delays and additional costs for completion. I was not entirely responsible for this, as authorities did not keep records regarding cable, gas, or electricity utility providers during those years. Invariably, someone from any of the authorities would be digging to lay a new cable and strike one without a record of its placement. Panic would ensue when a telephone cable, gas main, or electricity line was cut by one party or another, leading to a search for which cable it was and who was responsible for fixing it. This typically resulted in laying another cable rather than repairing the old one. The same applied to the coaxial cable for telephones laid across the harbour from north to south. When half of North Sydney suffered a major blackout or loss of telephone connections, a new cable was laid across the harbour from a barge. When the cross-city tunnel was constructed, they found a spaghetti of cables crisscrossing each other. The engineers laid the roadway under the harbour above those cables and opted for new lines again whenever a technical fault occurred.

Most of the decision-making regarding the approval of the cable laying for the phone line was done by me and a Divisional Clerk over a skin full of alcohol. The same applied to signing off on non-existent overtime for jobs, paying car duties, or missing mechanical aids. It was, after all, the public service. My most memorable experience of living dangerously was during a duty flying with a grounded pilot from Qantas. We navigated the skies in a small crop duster to determine the optimal locations for TV tower installations across the nation. The activity involved acrobatic displays such as Kimacazi's reckless dive bombing, pulling out at the last minute, flying into clouds, and rolling the aircraft on its side. I did not mind it so much as the sick feeling I had from the hangover the night before.

I never gave it much thought at the time, but I had a mentor in the government's electricity commission and another in the Postmaster General's Department. Additionally, I was offered an administrative position five grades higher than my current position in the Prime Minister's Department in Canberra. I foolishly turned it down because I didn't want to move to Canberra.

Not long after, I began to feel disenchanted with my job and decided to apply for a position as an Insurance Sales Representative with AMP, Australia's largest insurance company. It turned out to be a godsend, as I thrived at selling and earned a good income between drinks for the next six years. Early in my life, while selling life insurance, I saved enough money to take an extended three-month holiday in Europe. Thus began another perilous adventure.

I never figured out whether it was my way of overcoming a sense of depression or the ongoing quest for answers to life's riddle. Still, my weakness for extreme sports, speeding, drugs, and other risky behaviours has always been a blend of risk and novelty that draws me in. Psychologists call "novelty seeking" the practice of being a daredevil who is not just looking for thrills but seeking the unexpected. People with this trait are often impulsive and easily bored, but new experiences release a surge of pleasure chemicals in their brains.

When I look back on those days of intrepid behaviour, I wonder if I would have ever attempted any such activities had I been sober at the time. It took courage to overcome fear, but the fortification of too much alcohol in my system made it easy to do so. Did I do it out of ego recognition, bravado, a desire to prove myself invincible, to conquer dangers, to cheat death, or was it simply to take my mind off my depressive nature in an all-out effort to be present? It was all of those and more. It allowed me to gain recognition with women, as some are attracted to the daredevil for a good time, but don't view such a man as suitable husband material in the long run. Despite some who might protest, most women want a stable husband and a good father, and they're never as happy as when a large mortgage weighs down their man.

Ultimately, I settled into a responsible position as a sales manager, recruiting salespeople, which proved to be a key strength in my talents. For many years, all worked well, but risk-taking and gambling got in the way of a successful marriage. By this time, I was running my empire, which included a retail and wholesale store, as well as a nationwide supply of imports. I was riding high on the hog, so to speak, and everything I touched turned to gold before it ultimately proved too much for a dutiful partner, and the marriage ended after four children. I was back in the heap of loneliness, depression, and far too many alcoholic beverages that landed me in the hospital to dry out and embark on a new phase in my life, a journey inward.

A "journey inward" refers to the process of exploring one's thoughts, feelings, beliefs, and past experiences to gain a deeper understanding of oneself. It's a journey of self-reflection and introspection that leads to inner peace, knowledge, and alignment with one's true self. This journey can involve examining one's motivations, values, and core beliefs and can lead to a more profound sense of self-awareness and purpose.

Whilst much of my inner journey experience came at the cost of significant mental turmoil, pain, and suffering, it also involved nurturing my feelings on a slow path to recovery. It came with giving up alcoholic beverages and finding a pathway through the steps of Alcoholics Anonymous. Just as effective were the serpentine journeys in the context of adventure and exploration: travel experiences that prioritised remote, often under-surveyed, and pristine locations, while supporting my introduction to a new form of education. These journeys proved to be holistic, encompassing a variety of activities, including wildlife vistas, meeting people from diverse backgrounds and thus being educated in other cultures, experiencing moments of great natural awe, and discovering talents I never knew I had, thanks to my birthright.

The older man at the sidewalk cafe.

There's an old man
at the sidewalk cafe
drinking his coffee slowly
sitting there, taking it easy
No longer on the go.

Is that the old man
Who made a fortune
The hero of Big Dome and Co?
Didn't he see it crumble
Or did he just let it go?

Does the older man know the wisdom
sitting there, taking it slow
Watching the passing parade
learning to live and let go.

Oh! He knows his time is fading
The sunsets are kicking in
He can hear the bell tolling
Is it ringing just for him?

See the old man
at the sidewalk cafe
drinking his coffee neat
Lost in a dream of past glory
fading so slowly with him.

Does the old man know the wisdom
sitting there, taking it slow
Watching the passing parade
learning to live and let go.

CHAPTER 3

AWESOME EAGLES

It is a historical truth that when one is facing what seems to be insurmountable odds, the courage needed to "take flight" – to make a significant change or move forward – is a multifaceted blend of resilience, self-belief, and the willingness to embrace uncertainty. It involves recognising the value of taking risks, even when fear is present, and trusting in one's ability to navigate the unknown.

I am reminded of the methodology eagles use to teach their young to take flight. Eagles don't "force" their young to fly. Instead, they encourage their baby eaglets to leave the nest by withholding food, perching nearby with food, or flying with food to entice them to fly to a perch, all while vocalising and flying around the nest. The eaglets are generally eager to try their wings and don't require any forceful coaxing. Suffering from hunger and pain reinforces the eaglets' need to overcome the risks of falling and take to the air.

Once the mother Eagle is assured of the eaglet's ability to fly, she takes each eaglet by the scruff of the neck and flies to a great height, dropping the eaglet who flies away, never to return to the nest. If an eaglet keeps falling, the mother eagle swoops down and, once more, takes it to an incredible height, dropping it repeatedly until it overcomes its fear and flies away. Such is the way of nature, and that's why we see Eagles soaring in the skies, hunting for prey below to feed their young. The father must hunt and protect the nest against predators, and the mother must nurture, but both Father and Mother Eagles let go of their young once they have learn to fly.

We must learn to let go, let God, so to speak. Many aspects of nature teach us valuable lessons. I am reminded of a couple of instances where nature, through the influence of eagles, taught me the incredible power of nature during my recovery from incidents of suffering.

The first was after a heavy night on the grog when my defective nature took hold. I had been at a friend's house at the time. In my drunken cups, I got a bit too amorous with my mate's sister in his opinion. He encouraged me out of the house into the darkness of the back yard under the pretext of showing me something of interest. In the darkness, I could not see anything, but I soon felt the sharp blow of his fist on my chin, followed by a flurry of blows to the body. I was felled like an oak tree cut off at the base. In my drunken stupor, I didn't know what hit me. He was in the right, protecting his sister, but his methodology may have been a little too harsh. The next morning, with cap in hand, and a bruised body as a reminder of my mistake, I made my way to his sister and apologised. As to my mate, he had another idea: to make it up to me in his way. He soon appeared at my door with two fly fishing rods and invited me to go to a river in the bush with him to see if we could catch a fish or two.

Essentially, any fish that surface feeds on insects or small animals can be caught with a fly. If you are unfamiliar with fly fishing, the "bait" is a fly —a lightweight, artificial lure designed to mimic insects or other small aquatic creatures. These flies are attached to the end of the fly line and cast out onto the water. The joy of casting the line with rod and reel is a knack worthy of consideration. Even if you don't catch a fish, there is much peace and serenity in casting a line to fish.

So, after I recovered from my good friend's beating, he took pity on me and brought me fly fishing. Amazingly, I ventured upstream in one direction, while he went in the opposite direction to cast his line. It was so relaxing out there in nature, listening to the stream's flow alongside the silence, broken only by the whisper of the line as it glided across the water when casting. Then, as the silence returned, I heard the faint sound of a "swoosh, swoosh" upstream, growing louder as it approached me. Looking toward the sound, I saw a large eagle with its wings spread wide, soaring about a metre above the water, mid-river. It passed me with barely a glance and slowly rose into the early morning sun, like a large jumbo jet on takeoff. The sight of this natural occurrence lifted my mood into the present. A gift was indeed given to me by the nature of God.

I am reminded of an inspiring story that has circulated widely in the media for years. It tells the tale of an eagle's transformation and determination to survive. The broad appeal of this story highlights the eagle's extraordinary ability to captivate and inspire humans. While this narrative is uplifting and may encourage us to reflect on our life journeys, it is, after all, just a story. Biologically, it is not entirely accurate. The eagle has one of the most extended life spans among birds, typically ranging from 20 to 30 years in the wild. As apex predators, they possess a relatively long lifespan compared to many other birds. The oldest known wild eagle is approximately 32 years old.

Talons are hard, sharp and curved throughout the eagle's life. Talons and beaks are made of keratin, the same material as our fingernails. Think about how long it takes for your nails to grow. Its long and sharp beak becomes bent. An eagle's beak is hooked to rip and tear its food. Like all birds of prey, it has a distinctive hooked beak throughout its life. Beak and talons are critical to eagles' ability to catch and consume food. No eagle can survive without a beak or talons for any time. Due to its thick feathers, its old and heavy wings become stuck to its chest, making it challenging to fly. Feathers are replaced throughout an eagle's life, a process called moulting. An eagle does not lose all of its feathers at once; it is a gradual process that continually renews the feathers. Then, the eagle is left with only two options: die or undergo a painful 150-day change process. The process requires that the eagle fly to a mountain top and sit on its nest.

An eagle's nest is used solely for rearing its young. They only occupy their nest for a few months each year while raising their offspring. The eagle knocks its beak against a rock until it is plucked out. Both beak and talons are critical for eagles' ability to catch and consume food. No eagle can survive without a beak or talons. The eagle begins plucking its old feathers as its new talons regrow. An eagle cannot survive without food for more than two days. A few days without food might be feasible, but not longer. After five months, the eagle undertakes its famous flight of rebirth and can live for another thirty years. Reading the story evokes a positive feeling, but remember that it is biologically impossible for this narrative to be true.

It seems that eagles appear when moments of change are required in life, but sometimes we miss the significance of this phenomenon, realising only later the importance of their presence. Such was the occasion when I went on a road trip with my son Peter a couple of decades ago, before he took his own life. In many cultures, birds of prey, such as eagles and hawks, symbolise strength, power, and, at times, death or the spirit world. These associations can vary in interpretation based on individual beliefs and cultural backgrounds, and may exacerbate feelings of vulnerability or anxiety in specific contexts. Although there may be a symbolic or psychological connection between birds of prey and feelings of depression or anxiety, it is essential to recognise that the presence of birds of prey is a natural occurrence and should not be interpreted as a definitive sign of a mental health condition.

My son, Peter, and I drove my new four-wheel drive vehicle up the mountainside of Tasman National Park in Tasmania, known for its rugged coastline, which includes Australia's highest sea cliffs, unique geological features, and popular walks like the Three Capes Track. The park protects the eastern and southern coastal regions of the Tasman and Forestier peninsulas, offering a variety of natural attractions. We parked on a cold, crisp morning on a cliff edge overlooking the mountainous terrain. I had walked to the back of the vehicle and opened the boot to get another warm jacket. A shadow appeared behind me, and I turned to see a giant eagle with a vast wingspan. It hung in the air, no more than a meter, flapping its wing gently now and again without moving near or far from me. The eagle just stayed there, and I didn't move either. I asked Peter, sitting behind the wheel in the driver's seat, to look in the rearview mirror. Once the bird had more than made its presence felt, it slowly winged its way upward and vanished into the skyline.

Such incidents happened many times to Peter before the devastation of his depression took a turn for the worse, and he ultimately wrote a farewell letter to his family and died by his own hand. The breakdown of my marriage, loss of my son, family ties and loss of my material world left me with in-depth depression and anxiety. Part of my recovery involved returning to the bush for solace. It was there that I had many encounters with birds of prey. Eagles and black crows often came to visit me or hang about when at my lowest ebb. One may view it as a series of serendipitous events, but having been there and experienced so many of these 'coincidences,' I am more inclined to believe that they were more than coincidental; real lessons on living in the presence of God through natural occurrences.

Birds, particularly predators, are a natural reminder of the world's harsh realities, including the constant threat of predation and the struggle for survival. Such realities might trigger or amplify feelings of vulnerability and anxiety. It's also important to recognise that the appearance of birds of prey is a natural phenomenon that occurs randomly, and there may be no specific connection to a person's mental state. The encounter could be a coincidence.

I have had experiences with natural coincidences that evoke the essence of recovery and the beauty of the natural world. One such occasion was watching a school of dolphins herding fish, much like cattle being rounded up for market. Another was witnessing a significant whale breach near the shoreline and being so close that I could see the barnacles on its underside as it rose high out of the sea.

Similarly, I have had numerous encounters with snakes that came close to me, and I once trod on a venomous snake without getting bitten. One such incident occurred while I was walking in the bushland: a snake suddenly appeared in front of me on a bush track. It rose, coiling high on its tail, spinning in front of me, paused, and took a final look before returning to the bush. We often struggle, thinking all is lost, or have extreme expectations of what should be.

Nature teaches us that there is another way to operate a system—one based not on scarcity but on abundance and generosity. As ecosystems evolve, they become more diverse. This diversity creates more resources, not fewer, within a system. The pain of losing a family member, experiencing mental illness, or suffering a loss of material wealth is sometimes necessary to awaken us to the spiritual connection we all have with nature, allowing us to heal and move forward again. Indeed, the maturity we learn from creatures like the eagle, dolphin, or snake all serve as reminders to learn from nature rather than solely from the ways the world seems to offer us.

"Faith is the bird…."

There was once a broken little bird
Who lost the gift of flight,
Or so it seemed in the darkest hour,
The wind was not quite right.

How could the air in a storm or mist
Help a bird in flight?
How could he sing to other birds,
For there was none in sight?

So there he was, alone and lost
In sadness and doubt,
It was to this little bird,
What life was all about.

Our feathered friend rehearsed,
searched down memory lane,
praying not to be bound to earth,
that he might fly again.

To search, to chance some carefree way,
to jump and trust to fly,
The bird looked for an easy route,
so that this bird might fly.

But in the scary moments,
To unbelief prevailed,
So he began to doubt the truth,
For a flight to the bird was a fable.

In time, of course, the renewed bird,
Believed he was alright,
climbed to the highest mountain top,
there to attempt to flight.

So with courage before reason,
He jumped from this great height,
and with the help of wind and air,
This bird returned to flight.

"Faith is the bird that feels the height,
and sings while the dawns still dark."
                              -Lagone.

CHAPTER 4.

ACCEPTANCE

In my many trials of life, love and lust, pain and hardships, rejection and loss, I emerged from the long night of the soul of unbelief to an acceptance of something greater than myself—a force field of creative imagination and a logical understanding of the meaninglessness of it all without a power greater than myself to guide me. This came with the recognition of being a loner and an outsider, which is inherent within. It is a monumental discovery when we truly accept that we are born outsiders, genetically programmed to be as we are. Through this revelation of my life's journey, both for the present and with a vision for the future, it has become a source of peace, irrespective of circumstance.

I recall the guidance I received from a fellow patient during our hospitalisation in recovery from depression and anxiety a decade or so ago. He likes me, a sober alcoholic, struggling with the highs and lows of coping with life on life's terms. He encouraged meditation, taking it easy, going with the flow, and using no force.
"Go with the grain of life like a carpenter planing wood. If you go against the flow, you will only get splinters." I found the notes I had taken from his wisdom. The man has passed away, but I want to share the notes from our written conversations. The man was Doctor Kynear, a friend of Carl Jung: "Be open-minded, be willing to grow."

In the writing of these lines, I am thinking of the phrase "To thine own self be true," which was said by the character Polonius in Shakespeare's play Hamlet. It's a well-known line of advice Polonius gave his son, Laertes. The line advises a person to be true to themselves, implying that if one is honest with oneself, they will naturally be true to others. Polonius advises his son, "to thine own self be true," yet fails to follow his advice, betraying his morals through his actions.

For a time, I followed the many phrases of that man of spiritual brilliance until I had recovered enough from depression and anxiety to step out there again. Then, soon enough, I returned to the ways of the world, for more often than not, I took the well-worn path of pleasure and material goal seeking at the expense of my better nature. Too frequently, then not, I returned to the arms of a woman in preference to going to God.

So much of the wisdom of the spirit returns now as I turn over the pages of the notes I wrote down back then. Thursday 23/8/ 2007. Ceased drinking forty-seven days ago and went straight to rehab.
A note from Dr. Kynear: " There is a golden thread that runs through everything. It is a fact of nature that this is our connection to God." Then another note: " You require inner honesty with yourself. Open-mindedness and a willingness to grow."

I was mindful of the need for direction, courage, acceptance, and the will to grow. To go with the flow, there would be continuous moments of spiritual awareness. Acceptance means not to worry; it means living with whatever comes up. I needed, and still do, the synchronicity —the meaningful coincidences that led me on the path of well-founded virtue. I was conscious then of being gentle with myself, using no force, for the energy would flow with me in time. The lessons came slowly as they always seem to do. The one guiding influence I recall, like a mantra, that I have done my very best to be ever mindful of, was Dr. Kynear's 'go with the flow' philosophy.

"Go with the flow…put your boat of personality into the inner river of life and go with the current in the spiritual open waters. Once you get the drift of this, all it takes is just a gentle movement of the rudder to stay on course."

The other dark secret he taught me that has come to pass on numerous occasions, "Gradually surrender the ego, taking the risk to let go. You will come to a vacuum, the risk of letting go and falling into the dragon's mouth, into the pit where the dragon lives. It will blossom into a lotus flower of creative ideas, bringing inner calm and peace, and gradually restoring tranquillity. The answers will come not so much from without but within. You will let go of the past and learn acceptance. Stay detached. Ride out the anxiety… let go…easy does it." ….."Don't think, just be."

I am reminded that feelings are not real; they are just feelings. They are merely false evidence that appears real. If we hang on, they soon pass as well. Surrender, detach, and be at peace. Go with the grain of the timber, so to speak. Sometimes, when we are in a meditative state, the feelings are of nothingness; there is no-thing there. It is being with the presence of God, like being in the eye of the storm, where it is still, knowing that outside of this state, there is a tempest of a raging sea of life. The analogy I use here is that when faced with life's challenges, we slowly learn to detach, regardless of what is happening around us.

I recall the meditative lessons I learned while walking the Camino on my pilgrimages. I was learning to let go and be free, and in that state, I fell into the dragon's mouth; what emerged was a lotus flower of creative ideas. Over the last decade, I have written numerous books and songs, hoping that others will benefit from my imagined and real pursuits. However, I have found over time that it has been, to some extent, a crutch to further lessen the fall, like a residual parachute—a way of reducing the tension that remains within me to let go. For a time, I returned to alcohol to lessen the impact of the pain and suffering. I was still holding on to something I had not fully let go of. And then the lust after a woman to escape my real fears, a mountain to climb, or some other adventure of my own making, did not quell the fear of letting go absolutely. The residual parachute remains.

In the AA principles that I have come to believe in, there are four that are paramount to my remaining sober, and a worthwhile guide 1. We surrender to win. 2. We give way to keep. 3. We struggle to get well. 4. We die to live. The world offers the opposite to this. For we are destined to take the middle road, it can't be achieved by linear, rational, sequential, logical means. These are the ways of the world, the half-brained way. The way of the spirit and the imagination is the third way, tempered by our boat of personality floating on the waters of life, as I have alluded to before. We must learn to trim the sail, adjust the rudder of existence from within our spiritual core and go with the flow, for we are the seekers of the inner truth, which becomes the universal truth, that which Augustine famously stated: "Great are you, O Lord, and exceedingly worthy of praise; your power is immense, and your wisdom beyond reckoning. And so we men, who are a due part of your creation, long to praise you – we also carry our mortality about with us, the evidence of our sin and the proof that you thwart the proud. You arouse us so that praising you may bring us joy, because you have made us and drawn us to yourself, and our heart is restless until it rests in you."

There is within us all a flame, a symbol of life itself. If we care to listen, it speaks within: "Exist, stay alive, survive." A statement by Chinese philosopher Lao Tzu comes to mind: "In breathing in stillness of body and mind, an inner flame is born."

From time to time, I need to remind myself that I have an inner nature, an inner world, inner dignity, and inner nobility, which resonate with inner approval and reject the ways promoted by those of worldly influence, outward symbolism, in favour of inner spirituality. Indeed, I cannot change the circumstances of the past and my part in them. I am living now, and the influences that I embrace are what I come to accept as being in my best interest: of my body, mind, and spirit. My reality is that I live for others, and I also live for myself, but it must be done with discernment and knowledge that it is for the greater good, not some ego-driven notion.

Some other things that come to mind from my time in hospital recovery are: "The highest form of human intelligence is to observe without evaluation or judgment." And another: "When we sincerely try to connect with others, it is very powerful." Such a statement now resonates with the 12th Step of AA for me: "Having had a spiritual awakening as the result of these steps, we tried to carry this message to alcoholics, and to practice these principles in all our affairs."

Interestingly, we tend to react aggressively rather than engage in a peaceful interchange when someone challenges us. "Non-violent communication is to create a connection, not to get what you want." It's the opposite of what our egocentric nature suggests we do. Our attempts are futile if we resist our old thought patterns by fighting them. If we want to change the flow of our thoughts, all we need to do is introduce a trickle of new ideas that flow in a different direction, and surprisingly, a new pathway will open up on its own. All we have to do is step out there, and the doors will open. If we stop thinking, there is nothing we will not know; the journey has no distance.

We sense that we must have the illusion of time and space to pretend there's somewhere to go and something to do. A safety zone allows us to experience life and navigate through it. It's the experience of pleasure and pain, loss and gain, desire and shame, blame, fame; it's all the same, just a game. I now understand the wisdom in Jesus' words: "Be in the world but not of the world." We will never take the illusion game seriously again. We will become more like children, enjoying the exciting, beautiful things. As children, it was always just a game. Why did I miss that in my adult life?

What must I do to achieve this altered state of being?
Well, the only immediate thing to bring into effect is to have infinite patience. It involves a series of healthy thought patterns that I must remind myself of if I am destined to change. In doing so, however, I am reminded that it's not the words I write or utter, but rather the experience. I am willing to let go of who I am. For me, it's about experiencing whatever arises from the effects of my knowledge. The real me is the heart and soul of the essence of who I am. When feelings are not expressed, Doug is not being himself. The 'I' is the false self built over a lifetime. I've taken over myself with experiences, rather than expressions of the true self. Doug is a person. It's the intelligence. The real me is the heart of who I am. [It all seems so deep and meaningful, and it is.]

Love gone wrong through emotional confusion and psychological manipulation can create in an individual, who lacks full consciousness or emotional maturity, to see what is being done. In actions driven by uncontrolled desire, feelings of guilt, intense passion, and insecurity give rise to the possession of dark myth. We open the door to great suffering when we bring dependent feelings into a relationship. If we are to be fully alive to live through and cope with being separated from another, we need to endure. We will not be fully alive if we attempt to manipulate and bind. We must learn to hand over to a Higher power within, to shape our destiny, so we overcome the fear of being alone.

During my pilgrimages on the Camino de Santiago, I discovered many outward signs and symbols that guided me from the myths of the finite world to an infinite spiritual connection and completeness. The lessons I learnt on those perilous journeys set for me a template for living that, to a great degree, is lacking in our hedonistic lifestyle today. It meant I had to experience shadow myths to uncover enlightening truths, lessons of romantic lust to understand the foundations of love, let go of medications and turn to nature to cure mental abnormalities and unreal desire, to fulfil symbolic needs that can only be satisfied through the language of the heart.

The relationships of my past life tell of myths of passion and repulsion, marriage to ultimate separation, love and rivalry, sexual fidelity and infedelity, and the transcendent power of compassion which ultimately underlined the central importance of love in my life which is paramount to all humanity best form of living happy, joyous and free. Human relationships are so complex, and the morality of myths is equally multifaceted. The puzzle and mystery of what people are attracted to or repelled by each other requires great stretches of the soul to understand correctly.

The loves and sorrows of myths come in many shapes and colours; some are erotic. Although some of our life stories of love and sorrows may challenge many of our moral assumptions about relationships, myths about love can offer solace in our unhappiness, guidance in our dilemmas, and sorely needed insights into why we sometimes create the dilemmas we do in our personal lives.

CHAPTER 5.

SYMBOLS & SIGNS OF THE WAY

My Camino journeys opened a connection with my creative side. I had experienced the depths of despair due to the breakdown of my family, the suicide of my son, and the loss of material possessions and power with the forced closure of my business. These events, along with the death of two friends—one from a heart attack and the other from suicide—felt like the end of my life. Before taking that step forward on my first Camino, I had all but given up the will to live.

The conundrum of my life, the mystery of suffering and death, led me to seek answers through excessive consumption of alcohol and eroticism, leading to despair and the shadow self, which eventually brought me to a more profound sense of higher reality. The mysteries of the downward spiral of human enigma compelled me to seek life's fundamental meaning. I tried to resolve my dilemma through passionate encounters with women who, like me, had faced instability and pain in their lives. However, these relationships only deepened their suffering. The drink provided temporary relief from the symptoms, but it was merely a temporary solution that ultimately didn't work.

I did not know then that profound guidance would come with philosophical discussions related to my linear, logical approach to the Steps of AA, and later, the belief in a Higher Power that emerged through my imagination more than through the indoctrination of faith and morals from my Christian upbringing. It is not always easy to be enriched with elusive glimpses of meaning, allowing some constructive meaning to emerge from the frustrating passage I was on and the painful experiences I had to endure. I could have soon become bitter and twisted over my circumstances. In the state of mind I found myself in, I failed to grasp the profound levels of understanding and potential opportunities that could have been had in these crossroads I was to endure.

The coming to believe in a power great than self to hand over too though the AA programme, and my Camino de Santiago pilgrimages, lifes mysteries became paradoxical, mythical tales of which I was too encounter with powers that are greater than my self that would give me a broader vision than any science or conventional religious thinking could teach. It was within the community of AA, and on my journey on the Camino de Santiago, and time in recovery in rehab, that the strength of my human soul was called into being by the realisation that there is meaning, if not answers, embedded in that which I found most baffling in life.

Throughout my life, I had many different signs to steer me in the direction of life that would ultimately lead me to what my higher power had built into my destiny. Like most younger men, I ignored them in favour of my desires, in what I believed was my progressive realisation of a worthwhile predetermined goal. All proved ultimately to be of no value to me. The fulfilment of erotic desires, drunkenness, material possessions, pride in my achievements and some things that appeared to glitter wasn't gold and, on reflection, unnecessary to my better self and empty to my spirit.

Now I sit in awe and wonder about the many symbols and signs that offered spiritual guidance on my inner journey, such as cues or messages from the spirit world, intuition at the time, or wise guidance from loved ones who have passed over. These messages manifested in various forms, including visual imagery, auditory cues, or intuitive impressions. Recognising and interpreting these signs helped deepen my understanding of my spiritual path and connect with my higher self. They are more significant now than they seemed at the time of their occurrence. I remember in no particular order such signs and symbols, of which there were many on my Camino journeys. These timely happenings were given to me in my senior years, for my rite of passage was no longer that of my youthful years. So many of these occurred before I ventured forth on my adventure of the journey of the spirit, before I even thought about the Camino de Santiago.

Perhaps the most significant moment occurred when I joined a spiritual programme, a community-based discussion group called GROW. I was experiencing depression and anxiety after quitting drinking. It is a unique recovery program that offers mutual support for those with mental health issues. At the time, I didn't know it was based on the 12-step program of Alcoholics Anonymous, where I would later find my way. I had just left a session and was walking along a suburban street when I noticed a small object on the footpath. I picked it up, and it was a medallion. One side featured a walking staff similar to the one I used on my bush walks when I escaped into nature. The front depicted a man walking near a mountain path with two walking poles. Above him, a black crow flew away, and the man looked happy, joyous, and free. Surrounding the edge of the medallion was a river, and at the top, there was a small cross. It didn't make sense at the time, but the symbolism of the medallion would later resonate with my Camino journey.

On another occasion, about five hundred kilometres into my first Camino, I had stopped to rest on the side of The Way. It was late morning, a beautiful, clear day with no clouds in the sky. I was sitting with two other pilgrims of The Way, sharing some food and resting our bodies after letting go of the weight of our backpacks for a while before venturing out again. Then, from nowhere, a feather floated down from the sky. There was no bird nor bird's nest from a tree; it was just a clear blue sky out on an open plain. It represented divine guidance, an offer of protection from the spirit world. I had been suffering a lot from blistered feet; the fellow pilgrims had given me some soothing cream to rub on them before I once more ventured forth. In the next village, some eight kilometres away, I stopped for a cup of coffee and took off my boots again to ease my aching feet. I was out of painkillers in my medical kit and wished for some Voltaren tablets to relieve my pain and reduce inflammation in my feet. I had hardly had this thought when a couple I had encountered a day or two along the Way. I told them of my predicament, and without hesitation, they gave me half a packet of, you guessed it, Voltaren!

I am also reminded of my spiritual connection through my link with nature. During my long walks alone, before I embarked on the Camino, I often encountered guidance that offered some deep and meaningful lessons. I used to see faces in the natural creases in rocks worn by wind and rain. Later, I discovered that where I saw these faces, the Aborigines used to walk, and in some cases, they may have died there as well. In one instance, I walked along a not-so-frequented track and came across a sign carved into a rock. I took a photo of it and picked up a stick nearby using its notches to measure the various angles of what I perceived to be a plan of some sort. The multiple notches in the stick fitted exactly the contours of the etching in the rock. In my mind, a vision appeared redirecting the coastal river system inland, allowing the Darling River to be filled with water during droughts. Later, in researching drought, the same diagram was found to have been used to address inland drought in New South Wales, dating back to the 1930s. Amazing! Of course, these findings had no bearing on my life, but someday someone may have the same experience and take action to solve the drought problem using drawings and similar ideas. It goes to show that serendipitous events come our way. We can either act upon them or leave them to the universe to deal with at some point in the future.

The Tree of Life has always been deeply connected to spirituality. Jesus reportedly stated, "I am the vine, you are the branches." After suffering the loss of my son Peter at his hand, I wrote the epilogue for his funeral ceremony. It was a lengthy poem, but the crux of it was in the introduction: " I am the vine, you are the branches, some of us are branches, some of us are leaves, some falling leaves, and some fallen leaves and we all come under the power of the sun, and the Father, the Son and the Spirit are one." We all ultimately decompose like the leaves of a tree and return to the earth to revitalise the soil, starting the cycle of life again.

On my first Camino, I was still in much psychological pain, but the spiritual world came to me in another way. I had written a song about my Grandfather, which started as a poem. I met a rock musician on the route, and he asked me to send it to him as he wished to add music to it and record it for his next album. What ultimately flowed from that was a lotus flower of creative ideas. I had been given by the universe a means of expressing, in symbolic purity, a new connection to the spiritual world. Many songs and books have since catalysed the expression of what is going on inside me. For a time, they acted as a resilient parachute against the fearful dragon's mouth of reality, but now they represent a slow outpouring of my spiritual self for my well-being. [And hopefully yours too.]

The three Camino pilgrimages I undertook brought with them numerous coincidences, lessons of love and lust, ideas, and endless actions over the next decade that guided me to where I am now. In the process, I have come to understand my heart and developed feelings of understanding and respect for others, which have since evolved. Equally, I am more conscious than ever that the need to remain as vigilant as a female serpent and yet as innocent as a dove when dealing with the rest of humanity is paramount to my spiritual well-being and my continual journey inward.

There is a specific Yin-Yang representation of harmony and balance in using our creative talents for well-being. This sense of a newfound freedom of expression often comes after separation from those we love through loss, such as marital breakdown, or some other archetypal experiences. It is doubtful that any human being passes through life without some suffering to answer their dilemma of living life as they are meant to. Established religious practices have long sought to address the mystery of why we suffer, especially when the suffering appears unfair or unjust, and such answers, although often unsatisfactory to the inquiring mind, have provided some comfort over the ages to those seeking to alleviate their pain. Myth, however, unlike religious dogma, has never offered an answer about why we suffer, or how we may avoid it, or what God will give us in recompense.

On the other hand, the transformative effect of suffering may be glimpsed in many myths, suggesting that some deep purpose or function lies embedded in those experiences which tell stories of separation and loss, for in them we may discover a mirror of our circumstances, and realise that we are not alone if we consider deeply enough the perspective offered in myth and symbolism, too, that the only true healing for human suffering arises from human sharing and compassion, rather than specious, easy answers which profess to explain away one of life's greatest enigmas.

Life is not for me, or you, dear reader, a Hollywood fantasy. As such, evil often goes without being punished, and the good guy is gunned down or unmercifully punished. It seems unfair that talented young people are usually the ones who suffer the most. Some young people die before they have barely lived at all. We see ruthless dictators, responsible for thousands of murders, live to a ripe old age and die comfortably in their sleep. This stark dimension of life has provided fuel for millennia of religious controversy. Although the precise definition of goodness continues to elude even the most self-righteous of spiritual teachers, we humans persist in the hope that, if we could only discover the formula, we would escape life's vicissitudes.

Often, belief in certain practices, while bringing enlightenment to followers, can also lead to significant pain and sadness within a culture associated with a geographical location. A prime example is the violent suppression of the 100 million people in China who practice Falun Dafa, also known as Falun Gong, a spiritual discipline rooted in ancient Chinese tradition. It combines gentle exercise and meditation centred on truthfulness, compassion, and forbearance. This practice has been shown to produce numerous health benefits, including increased energy, mental clarity, and stress relief. Unfortunately, for over 70 years, the Chinese Communist Party has employed violent measures to eradicate China's traditional culture and replace it with the communist ideal of atheism. Millions of Falun Gong practitioners in China have endured harassment, abduction, imprisonment, torture, and even death in custody for embracing this ancient, Buddhist-like enlightening lifestyle. Suffering can arise not only from cosmic forces beyond our understanding but also from the actions of individuals who inflict pain upon others through indoctrination and control, as they fail to see the wood for the trees.

In the Bible's story of Job, we see that the roots of human suffering and inequality don't lie in something as simple as sinning and, therefore, merited punishment. It all stemmed from a challenge from Satan to God. Their strange and disturbing dialogue reveals a cosmic realm devoid of the kind of morality that humans try to wrap themselves in, hoping for a heavenly reward. There is no logic, compassion, or reason in God's willingness to hand Job's fate over to Satan, except for the fact that Satan has stung Him with the suggestion that Job will lose his faith if God is not kind to him. In my trials, like Job, I suffered and ultimately lost faith. In my disbelief, I stood before the abyss and almost took my own life, but somehow, fate intervened, and I was pulled back from that path. I disbelieved for a time, but eventually, God overcame Satan's depressive influence because I learnt to trust in the slow work of God. Despite the less-than-attractive dimension of the divine presence in the biblical story, Job does not question the nature of God, nor the majesty of His presence. God is what God is, and no solution for the enigma of suffering can be found by trying to discover where Job's secret character defect lies that caused his suffering. For that matter, upon analysis of my own 'Job-like experience' of deep suffering, where my world fell apart, there seems to me now no reason for my suffering other than that it was and is a part of my life's journey. God, in His mercy, allowed my suffering. He didn't inflict it upon me; it was perhaps ordained in the cosmos, I don't know. The religious indoctrination of God that I was brought up in did not prepare me for the suffering I endured. Still, the experience shattered my egocentric view of life, instilling a humbling belief in life's mysteries that can only be discovered through the passage of pain, loss, and profound questioning of faith, as well as an acceptance of life's harsh reality.

Like Job, friends meant well during my great suffering, but offered only shallow viewpoints that did not touch the depth of my sorrow. Their consultative advice meant well, but analysing their opinions alone, perhaps, only exacerbated their in-depth fears, yet was of little help to me. I ultimately found relief in rest and silence, and I wanted to help those who suffer the burden of being an alcoholic. We learn that simple solutions and promises of future relief from present suffering do not compare with faith in a divine presence, for we cannot answer cosmic mysteries.

What happened to Job and his family could not be undone, although he was restored to sanity, regained his wealth, and had a new family. We cannot erase the past, magically heal our wounds, or eradicate our memories. What Job experiences made him perhaps more of a man than before his tragic pear-shaped life experiences? We see in Job a maturing process that we must endure sooner or later. Life's unfairness will touch us sooner or later, and we must undergo a process to come out the other side. If nothing else, it will keep us on a path of spirituality, wise to the artificial ways of the world compared to the ways of the spirit, that of what we are destined to be. Only after enduring pain and suffering like Job are we restored to be rooted in a belief in God, or find that what springs from faith is the potential to achieve great things for the greater good of all concerned. Only then can we be restored to ourselves and find the strength to renew our lives after suffering and loss.

It is in living life on life's terms. Despite our joys and disappointments, and even in the face of unhappy circumstances, we refrain from getting carried away with anything, leaving guidance to God alone so that we can see our way clear to be happy, joyous, and free. After all, he runs the show, not us.

Leela, Leela. This world is just a game. Winners lose, and losers win; the game is still the same. Leela, Leela, this life is just a play. Those who say don't know, and those who know don't tell. A baby's eyes see everything from under; the eyes of a young man see his lady's face with wonder. The eyes of an older man look upon the flowing river. What of those whose eyes are one? They leave this world forever.

CHAPTER 6.

THE SPIRITUAL QUEST

I have always been in search of something that is beyond reach. I have touched on it occasionally: a deep and meaningful purpose unique to me, like all humanity. Something is yearning within the human soul that never ceases to aspire to something greater than self, nor ever relinquishes its hold, that something eternal beyond the mortal body's death. It is the most tremendous difference between us and the other animals with whom we share this earthly realm. It is not just a simple desire to serve God, for it can be a quest for knowledge, not only of the divine as expressed in religious doctrinal terms, but also a kind of understanding of the laws of the universe that underpin the reality of what the world's most outstanding scientists and psychologists pursue. The quest for knowledge may lead us down dark paths of shadowy complexities and equally reveal to us the great sunlight, or expose us to the evil that lies within as much as it does to the good. The myths I uncovered on my life's journeys deal with the spiritual quest and involve self-confrontation, which throws into sharp relief the profound paradox of dark and light, for my inward journey as it does for the mythical and the stories that follow.

Duplicity bothers every human being who has ever lived. It is a mysterious battle between what is good in every human and what is evil. From my life's experience, we finally come to terms with who we are when we do the work to peel back our very nature, let go and pray for the release from our defects of character, and tread a new inner spiritual route. This journey takes us through the arid landscape of earthly pleasures. Through remorse and compassion, we come to comprehend both the darkness within our being and the light that lies within the order of the soul, ultimately finding inner peace. So with the mythical tale of Marlowe's tragic story of Dr. Faustus, I retell this epic example of good in its bewildering connection to evil.

Once, there was a brilliant philosopher and theologian named Dr. Faustus. Through his in-depth understanding and studies, he realised that the nature of God and the meaning of life could not be fully understood or satisfied by intellectual inquiry. A proud man was he, and with his excellent knowledge, he desired to uncover the answer to lifes riddle; the great mysteries he sought to discover through his efforts and not through the understanding of wiser heads than his, for he aimed to uncover the secrets of the universe and claim them for his own, and as ego will, take the credit.

It wasn't long before Dr. Faustus abandoned his theology studies and turned to the shadowy magic of a hermit. There, he could explore alchemical experimentation to uncover forbidden knowledge of magic and sorcery passed down from the ancient Egyptians. He had forgotten the biblical story of Adam and Eve, who ate fruit from the Tree of Knowledge, and the fate of the cursed race of humanity since that fateful fall. Yet, despite his efforts, even with forbidden research, he could not teach himself what he wished to know, and so he fell into a melancholy state, calling on the infernal spirits in his despair. By chance, a black dog mysteriously appeared at his summons in his study and then metamorphosed into a strange figure who announced himself as Mephistopheles, biblically speaking, the devil's messenger—a creature embodying the spirit of evil and contradiction. One who is always on the lookout for human souls to win over to darkness, thus cheating God, and Faustus desired this creature's knowledge of the secrets of life and the nature of the divine. And so, a pact was made between them, signed in blood; Mephistopheles agreed to serve Dr. Faustus in this world while Faustus agreed to serve Mephistopheles in the next. The cunning evil one knew full well the price Faustus would pay, but the philosopher had not realised that it was his immortal soul he was signing away for eternity.

For a time, Faustus was thrilled by the magic and mysteries unveiled before him, believing he was finally on the brink of uncovering God's secrets. However, over time, the dark spirits of negation gradually eroded the scholar's will, luring him deeper into sensuality and pride, causing him to lose all sense of a spiritual quest. Faustus met a young girl named Gretchen, whom Mephistopheles cunningly lured into the scholar's grasp. She became pregnant by Faustus, and when he abandoned her, she went mad, killed the infant in despair, and was subsequently executed for her crime. Realising the terrible destruction he had inflicted on an innocent life, Faustus felt deep and bitter remorse. Although he was in Mephistopheles's clutches, he had genuinely begun to love the girl, and thus, something in his soul remained immune to corruption. This was something Mephistopheles had not anticipated, as the redemptive power of love contradicted the evil one, who was unaware of it.
But such was the power of Mephistopheles's hold over Faustus for many years, and the philosopher indulged in every sensual pleasure and penetrated every secret mystery. He learned all he had wanted, known, and understood: heaven's glorious heights and the underworld's shrouded bowels. However, the remorse over Gretchen grew like a cancer inside him, and despite his corruption, something within him continued to grow too long in the shadows. As the scholar grew older, Mephistopheles waited with patience

and satisfaction, for the time would soon arrive when the scholar would face death, and then his soul would belong to the darkness.

But at the final moment, when Faustus at last confronted the actual consequences of the pact he had made, he was so filled with remorse and loathing that his soul slipped out of Mephistopheles' grasp, and he was borne aloft to heavenly splendour.

This story of Dr. Faustus, although a mythical tale, explores the struggle of every human to find the light amidst darkness. His narrative presents a paradox for us all, as we grapple with the conflict between our egocentric desires and our yearning to serve something greater than ourselves. Faustus embodies the questing spirit within every individual, courageous and individualistic enough to reject the dogma of faith and morals presented by conventional religions, yet dangerously arrogant in believing it can defy fundamental human morality in the name of knowledge. While we may condemn Faustus for his greed and arrogance, we must also admire his courage and willingness to risk his soul to uncover the heart of life's mysteries. Here, we encounter the profound paradox of good and evil. To acknowledge this truth, we must first confront it in the hidden darkness of our hearts.

Dr. Faustus's disillusionment with philosophical and theological offerings reflects the dilemma of a keen intellect that cannot simply accept what it is told to believe. If truly heartfelt, the spiritual quest does not arise from childlike acceptance of belief but from disillusionment and a profound desire to understand life's paradoxes. Many people remain in childlike faith, and in this comfort zone, have simple answers to moral and spiritual dilemmas; whilst they may risk no dangers inwardly, they can never honestly know what life is about, nor find any peace when confronted with unanswerable questions like those faced by the medieval Christendom of Faust's time. Questioning involves danger, requires courage, and opens up the potential for an authentic experience of the soul and inner world.

We learnt from Faust that power corrupts, a fact no less true for the spiritual realm than for the material one. Faust's newfound power pushed him over the moral edge, rendering him impervious to the destruction he inflicts on the innocent child, Gretchen. Yet, he does love her and cannot entirely ignore what he has done; that little sense of remorse, born from compassion, ultimately allows him to 'cheat' the Devil and find forgiveness and redemption. It is not his 'good works' that save him, but rather the fact that, despite being steeped in pride and sensuality, he can still love and feel remorse. We ought to be good in thought and deed if we are to be acceptable in the eyes of God. Yet, the story of Faustus teaches us that goodness is relative to the definition of morality espoused by any society at any epoch in history. Love and remorse, however, are not confined to doctrines of faith or any specific culture. They allow us to experience both the light and the darkness while retaining the soul's integrity. It is possible that any spiritual quest will lead us into our potential for darkness and destruction, and that through facing these things, we might even feel, for a time, that we are irredeemable – our own 'pact with the devil' – we experience what might be called grace. It is not just a term limited to Christianity; it is a mysterious inner release that arises from within and makes sense of our goodness and evil.

Faustus is not merely a simple morality tale; it represents an inward journey, akin to all myths, when viewed on a psychological level. All the characters reside within each of us. Faustus and Mephistopheles are two sides of the same coin, reflecting two dimensions of the human experience. We must embrace the Mephistopheles within ourselves when we feel disillusioned with life. In Goethe's great drama, Mephistopheles says to Faust: "I am the spirit which wills forever evil yet does forever good." Thus, it is within our inner darkness that we ultimately find our way to the light. Therefore, we walk the tightrope between the two alternatives. It is not a rush or a quick step, but a slow, careful movement, one step at a time.

In summary, I am reminded of the words of Cardinal John Henry Newman, living on the tightrope of my existence. He wrote the poem "The Pillar of the Cloud" while recovering from a fever on a boat trip.

Lead, Kindly Light, amidst the encircling gloom,
Lead Thou me on!
The night is dark, and I am far from home.
Lead Thou me on!
Keep Thou my feet; I do not ask to see
The distant scene; one step is enough for me.

I was not ever thus, nor prayed that Thou.
Should lead me on;
I loved to choose and see my path, but now I don't.
Lead Thou me on!
I loved the garish day, and, spite of fears,
Pride ruled my will. Remember not past years!

So long Thy power hath blest me, sure it still.
Will lead me on.
O'er moor and fen, o'er crag and torrent, till
The night is gone,
And with the morn, those angel faces smile,
Which I have loved long since, and lost a while ago!

The Buddha's enlightenment is a pivotal event that helps us gain a deeper understanding of the meaning of suffering and its ultimate purpose. Buddha's enlightenment is a profound religious parable that conveys the essence of suffering and the ultimate purpose of life. Drawing from what is known—be it myth, religious doctrine, or a human soul's actual journey—it exemplifies why the human soul's journey transitions from the darkness of ignorance to the transformative power of understanding within the cycle of life and death.

While the details of Siddhartha Gautama's life, later known as the Buddha, are debated and may be embellished in religious texts, archaeological and textual evidence strongly suggests that a historical Buddha existed. This evidence includes inscriptions from the 3rd century BCE, specifically Ashoka's Edicts, which mention the Buddha and Buddhism, including the Buddha's birthplace at Lumbini. Additionally, the discovery of a tree shrine at Lumbini, radiocarbon dated to the 6th century BC, predates other known Buddhist sites by at least 300 years, providing concrete evidence of Buddhism's existence before the time of Ashoka.

Much of what has been written is mythical, but according to tradition, the historical Buddha lived from 563 to 483 B.C., although scholars postulate that he may have lived as much as a century later. He was born to the rulers of the Shakya clan, hence his appellation Shakyamuni, which means "sage of the Shakya clan." The legends that grew up around him hold that both his conception and birth were miraculous. His mother, Maya, conceived him after she had a dream in which a white elephant entered her right side. She gave birth to him while standing, grasping a tree in a garden. The child emerged from Maya's right side fully formed and took seven steps. Once back in the palace, he was presented to an astrologer who predicted that he would become either a great king or a great religious teacher, and he was given the name Siddhartha ("He who achieves His Goal"). His father, evidently thinking that any contact with unpleasantness might prompt Siddhartha to seek a life of renunciation as a religious teacher, and not wanting to lose his son to such a future, protected him from the realities of life.

The ravages of poverty, disease, and even old age were therefore unknown to Siddhartha, who grew up surrounded by every comfort in a sumptuous palace. At age twenty-nine, he made three successive chariot rides outside the palace grounds and saw an older adult, a sick person, and a corpse, all for the first time. On his fourth trip, he encountered a wandering holy man whose asceticism inspired Siddhartha to follow a similar path in search of freedom from the suffering caused by the endless cycle of birth, death, and rebirth. Because he knew his father would try to stop him, Siddhartha secretly left the palace in the middle of the night and sent all his belongings and jewellery back with his servant and horse. Completely abandoning his luxurious existence, he spent six years as an ascetic, attempting to conquer the innate appetites for food, sex, and comfort by engaging in various yogic disciplines. Eventually, near death from his vigilant fasting, he accepted a bowl of rice from a young girl. Once he had eaten, he realised that physical austerities were not the means to achieve spiritual liberation. At a place now known as Bodh Gaya ("enlightenment place"), he sat and meditated all night beneath a pipal tree. After defeating the forces of the demon Mara, Siddhartha became a Buddha ("enlightened one") at thirty-five.

The Buddha continued to sit after enlightenment, meditating beneath the tree and standing beside it for several weeks. During the fifth or sixth week, he was beset by heavy rains while meditating, but was protected by the hood of the serpent king Muchilinda. Seven weeks after his enlightenment, he left his seat under the tree. He decided to teach others what he had learned, encouraging people to follow a path he called "The Middle Way," which emphasises balance rather than extremism. He delivered his first sermon in a deer park in Sarnath, on the outskirts of Benares. He soon gathered many disciples and spent the next forty-five years travelling around northeastern India, spreading his teachings. Although the Buddha presented himself only as a teacher and not as a god or object of worship, he is said to have performed many miracles during his lifetime. Traditional accounts relate that he died at the age of eighty in Kushinaga after ingesting a poisoned mushroom dish prepared by a hermit who was unaware that the mushrooms were tainted. Historically, it has been reported that the Buddha was intuitively aware of his impending death and that he would be poisoned, yet he still ate the dish prepared for him. His body was cremated, and the remains were distributed among groups of his followers. These holy relics were enshrined in large hemispherical burial mounds, some of which became essential pilgrimage sites.

Throughout the ages, it has become evident that the Buddha's enlightenment has provided wisdom to millions of believers. You don't have to be a Buddhist to get this. Siddhartha's first attempt to answer the inner journey questions by exposing the conventionally accepted rants is a common approach in many spiritual quests. Yet we are committed to truth as Siddhartha is, and not merely seeking comfort for our suffering, and we may find that such offerings cannot satisfy us. So we look further for answers outside the teachings of established religious structures.

Siddhartha then attempted to achieve spiritual enlightenment by denying his physical needs and desires. These alternative practices often represent a stage along the path for many people, who perceive that the physical body is the root of all evil and that physical pleasure interferes with spiritual life. Yet Siddhartha realised that he had to reject conventional religious doctrine, because the life of the body is also divine, and it is foolish at best and arrogant at worst to imagine we can find God by denying or even destroying God's creation. Psychologically, wholeness rather than extreme imbalance is the ideal toward which the sensible individual aspires, for the spirit cannot live when the body is wretched and ill. Sometimes we have to discover this through hard lessons, as Siddhartha did.

When he finally allowed himself to accept a bowl of rice and bathe in the river, his more rigid-minded disciples left him. In some way, we might find ourselves outcast from an easily established religious path if we live contrary to the dogma and acknowledge the need for our desires, which have been labelled 'evil or sinful. ' The great symbol of the Tree of Wisdom, under which Siddhartha achieves enlightenment, echoes the image of many myths. The Tree of Knowledge, found in the story of Adam and Eve, and the Tree of Immortality, which lies at the bottom of the sea and beckons in another mythological tale, are both represented in the World-Tree Yggdrasil, which holds up the cosmos in Norse and Teutonic myth. It is no coincidence that human imagination has envisaged the course of life and wisdom as a tree over the millennia. Perhaps this is because the tree embodies a fundamental duality at the core of the human soul; its roots are in the earth, but its branches reach for the heavens. And it is a living thing, not an artificial construction, and the spiritual truths Siddhartha seeks can be found only through such contact with organic life.

Unlike Faustus, Siddhartha focuses inwardly, rendering him immune to the demon's threats. Siddhartha's absolute serenity reflects the total commitment to his quest. It is an issue of focus, of priorities, and of giving central importance to the mysteries of contemplation. We will find no contemplation if we are distracted from our inner demons, be they physical temptations, fear and anxieties, or a state of mind rather than a prescribed set of principles. Perhaps this is why the Buddha alone could achieve what he did; such a focus on the importance of the inner world comes easily to us, especially when we are young. Intense inner effort of this kind may only be possible in the second half of our life, when we are weary beyond the point of satisfaction, and the sufferings of others may move us more than our small worldly pleasures and pains. Siddhartha tried every stage of life's experiences, each of which was necessary to move him to the next stage. He had to try everything before he was ready to relinquish the enlightenment that he was seeking.

Whether we perceive Siddhartha's enlightenment as an anamorphic image or his guidance as a religious avatar, the Buddha serves as a paradigm rather than an ordinary mortal. The lesson is to understand from a broader perspective, with an awareness of the causes and effects underlying much of human suffering. It may be possible for all of us if we're willing to quietly and unobtrusively pursue our quest for understanding at the core of our lives.

Mending a broken man.

Don't know how to tell you this
always thought it would be bliss
You checked out before your time
Now I'm just a broken man.

Why did you have to leave that way
Like a passing cloud, it just fades away
I still miss you every day
Can this broken man be mended?

Nobody knows what's coming down the pike
could be desolation
maybe it's pure light…

Everything is a blessing,
Everything is a curse
when I look in the mirror for answers,
See myself in reverse.

Somebody said to pray to Jesus,
Hand it over to the man
There's a sadness in this broken world
We must try to make it right.

It's time now for a new beginning
Embrace the heart, rebuild it all
Help this Humpty Dumpty man
climb back up upon the wall.

Everything is a blessing,
Everything is a curse
When I look in the mirrors for answers
I see myself in reverse.

CHAPTER 7

ENLIGHTMENT

Enlightenment is a philosophical movement and a state of spiritual realisation. As an intellectual movement, it emphasised reason, science, and individual autonomy, challenging traditional authority and promoting ideas like liberty, equality, and tolerance. In a spiritual context, enlightenment often refers to a state of awakening, a deeper understanding of reality, and a transcendence of ordinary experience. As mystics and philosophers throughout history have discovered, it comes with a knowledge of pain and suffering.

In consideration of enlightenment, we must not overlook Confucius. Also referred to as Kong Qui or K'ung Fu-tzu, he was a Chinese philosopher, teacher, and political figure, widely regarded as the father of Eastern thought. His teachings emphasised the creation of ethical social relationships, the establishment of educational standards, and the promotion of justice and honesty. His social philosophy was founded on the principle of *ren*—loving others—and he believed this could be realised through the Golden Rule: "What you do not wish for yourself, do not do to others." He died after being heartbroken by the death of a beloved son.

In exploring this aspect of being, we cannot bypass the great philosophers and what they stood for to enhance our reasoning on enlightenment, for it is through their teaching that we come to terms with our own 'Lightbulb moments' of inspiration, reason, and understanding of our philosophies and purpose for living in today's world.

To begin with, we will explore the intellectual marvels of ancient Greece and the influential thinkers who paved the way for Western philosophy. As a catalyst, we blend one of the oldest subjects in the world—philosophy—with a forward-looking mindset. We thus journey back in time to explore the foundational ideas that have shaped Western thought, laying the groundwork for the intellectual landscape we inhabit today. These early philosophical pillars continue to inform and inspire our understanding of the world, making them invaluable touchstones for navigating the challenges of tomorrow. So, let's delve into the ancient foundations that have propelled us forward and discover how philosophy remains a catalyst for progress, as well as those moments of understanding that lead us to the present age of enlightenment, our particular journey in today's world. Before we consider their lives, it is worth delving a little into the life of the earliest Avatar, who sought enlightenment through understanding the suffering of humanity and a commitment to endure.

The previous chapter explored the Buddha's journey, philosophy, suffering, enlightenment, and teachings on steering the middle way in our spiritual quest. Now, let us examine the great philosophers of ancient times.

The documented history of philosophy is often said to begin with Socrates, who, due to his notable teaching methods and the manner and circumstances of his death, was the first in a line of prominent men of great learning who died under noteworthy circumstances.

Socrates, the iconic philosopher of ancient Greece, firmly believed that pursuing knowledge was the pathway to leading a virtuous life. Because he could neither read nor write, his students, Plato and Xenophon, recorded much of what we know about his life from around 470 BC to 399 BC. He revolutionised philosophical discourse with his unique Socratic method, an inquiry-based approach that skilfully exposed ignorance and challenged assumptions by engaging in relentless questioning and critical examination. He would have been aware of the Buddha, his philosophy of life, and his teachings on enlightenment. He was surely alive when the Buddha ate the poisonous mushroom. It is postulated that the Buddha was aware that he was being poisoned but still chose to suffer and die.

Socrates died in Athens in 399 BC after a trial for impiety, as he was accused of corrupting the youth. He spent his last day in prison among friends and followers who offered him a route to escape, which he refused. He died the next morning, following his sentence, after drinking a poisoned cup of hemlock tea. Like the Buddha, it was claimed that he knew it would kill him, yet he drank it rather than escape into exile or give up his beliefs. Socrates was not portrayed as intensely religious, but his philosophical dialogue often referred to divinities and expressed reverence for a higher power.

Interestingly, Isocrates (born 436 BCE in Athens—died 338 BCE in Athens) was an ancient Athenian orator, rhetorician, and teacher whose writings serve as an essential historical resource on the intellectual and political life of Athens during his time. While Isocrates promoted public life and prepared students for political engagement in the city's governance through his work, he often specifically highlighted those who excelled in relevant fields. In contrast, Socratic dialogues emphasise the significance of self-knowledge and advocate for a private study of true virtues in life.

While most scholars view Isocrates as a staunch rival to Plato, Aristotle, and other Socratics, it is beneficial to consider Isocrates and his contemporaries as negotiating the Socratic legacy while developing their unique approaches to education and philosophy. This perspective will show that Isocrates' portrayal of Socrates was more combative and critical than previously suggested. Isocrates reportedly starved himself after the Battle of Chaeronea in 338 BCE. He was deeply disillusioned by the loss of Greek independence and the rise of Macedonian dominance under Philip II. He had dedicated his life to advocating for Greek unity and peace under a strong leader, believing this was key to securing their future. The Battle of Chaeronea, in which Philip II defeated the combined Greek forces, shattered these hopes and led Isocrates to despair, ultimately resulting in his death by starvation. He was 98 years of age and reportedly happily married at the time.

Empedocles was a Greek philosopher renowned for his belief that all matter is composed of four elements: fire, air, water, and earth. Some have regarded him as the inventor of rhetoric and the founder of the science of medicine in Italy.

Empedocles was wildly popular in his day, and his visits to various towns were lauded as those of the wisest men. Alas, this popularity went to his head. While he did not incorporate the concept of gods into his theories, he began to consider himself a god, and he certainly wanted others to believe it. Legend has it that he jumped into a volcano to prove to his disciples that he was invulnerable to harm. He thought he would return as a god after being consumed by the fire when he leapt to his death into the crater of Etna in 435 BCE.

Aristotle (384–322 BCE), who follows Socrates and Plato as the third member of the great triumvirate of ancient Greek philosophers, is arguably the most critical thinker who ever lived.
Greek philosopher Plato (428-348 BCE) was a student of Socrates and later became a teacher of Aristotle. He was a *priori*, a rational philosopher who sought knowledge logically rather than from the senses. He established the Academy in Athens, one of the first institutions of higher learning in the Western world. Plato's logic explored justice, beauty, and equality, encompassing discussions of aesthetics, politics, language, and *cosmology*—the science of the origin and development of the universe. He died of a stomach disease in 322 BCE.

Considered one of the greatest thinkers in politics, psychology, and ethics, Aristotle learned from Plato after enrolling in his Academy at age seventeen. Later, he went on to tutor Alexander the Great. Aristotle focused on a *posteriori* routes of knowledge, a term popularised by Immanuel Kant, in which conclusions are formed based on actual observation and data. Aristotle's intellectual knowledge spanned every known field of science and arts, prompting him to idealise the Aristotelian syllogism, a belief that logical argument applies deductive reasoning to arrive at a conclusion based on two or more propositions assumed to be true.

Dante (1265-1321) was a Medieval Italian poet and moral philosopher regarded as the father of the modern Italian language. He is best remembered for his poetic trilogy, *The Divine Comedy*, which consisted of sections representing three tiers of the Christian afterlife: purgatory, heaven, and hell. The poem features an array of learning, an analysis of contemporary problems, and creativity in language and imagery. Dante's important theoretical works included discussions of rhetoric in the context of moral philosophy and political thought.

Blaise Pascal (1623-1662 was a French mathematician, physicist, and religious philosopher who laid the foundation for the modern theory of probabilities, a branch of mathematics concerned with analysing random phenomena. In 1657, Pascal published *Les Provinciales* under the pseudonym Louis de Montalte, a series of eighteen letters that defended Jansenism against the theology of the Jesuits.

John Locke was an English philosopher and Enlightenment thinker, widely regarded as the Father of classical liberalism. Throughout his studies, he made significant contributions to modern theories of limited, liberal government. His most notable work, *Essay Concerning Human Understanding*, analyses the human mind and its acquisition of knowledge. He also propagated a religious doctrine that taught the experience of God through the heart rather than through reason, which contrasted with the beliefs of the French philosopher René Descartes. Locke's thinking emphasised the idea that we should acquire knowledge through our experiences in the world. His logic later influenced philosophers such as Voltaire and Rousseau.

François Arouet (1694-1778), better known by his pen name "Voltaire," is widely regarded as one of the greatest French Enlightenment writers. He produced thousands of letters, books, pamphlets, essays, and plays, among other forms of writing, centred on religion and politics. One of his most famous works was *Candide*. This satirical novella pokes fun at the philosophical optimism proclaiming that all disaster and human suffering are part of a benevolent cosmic plan. According to one story **about French** philosopher Voltaire's last words, his response to a priest at his deathbed urging him to renounce Satan was, "Now is the time for making new enemies."

Immanuel Kant (1724-1804) was a German philosopher whose thinking centred on *metaphysics*, a philosophical discipline that examines the fundamental nature of reality. His best-known work, *Critique of Pure Reason*, determines the limits and scope of metaphysics by combining reason with experience, thereby moving beyond the traditional boundaries of philosophy. Kant was one of the foremost thinkers of the Enlightenment, and a large part of his work addresses the question, "What can we know?" Kant argued that we can only know things that are possible to experience. Further, he believes that we can understand the natural, observable world, but we cannot have answers to many of the most profound questions of metaphysics. In a work published the year he died, Kant analyses the core of his theological doctrine into three articles of faith: (1) he believes in one God, the cause of all good. In the world. (2) he believes in the possibility of harmonising God's purposes with our greatest good; and (3) he believes in humankind.

Simone de Beauvoir (1908-1986) is a French writer, existentialist philosopher, and social theorist who paved the way for the modern feminist movement. She published countless fiction and nonfiction works, often with existentialist themes. Her most notable book, *The Second Sex*, discusses the treatment of women throughout history and the oppression they endured. While her novels focused on existential themes, de Beauvoir's philosophies were heavily influenced by Karl Marx's historical materialism and Immanuel Kant's idealism. Beauvoir died of pneumonia on 14 April 1986 in Paris, aged 78. She is buried next to Sartre at the Montparnasse

Cemetery in Paris. She was honoured as a figure at the forefront of the struggle for women's rights around the time of her passing.

Now, I could write about many other philosophers and great minds. The purpose here is more to consider those who, by their beliefs and teachings, either advanced the cause of humanity, the journey of the human soul, and died for a reason or, in their interest, suffered the fate of any lost soul caught up in egocentric thinking to their detriment.

The myths, the lives, and the stories teach us that it is more productive to live our lives to the fullest and experience the richness of living every day, regardless of our material circumstances or desire to live a spiritual life, before we spend so much time trying to outwit death. And, in many ways, the fear of death, which is the same as a fear of life, for if we are unable to live in the present fully and are unwilling to accept our mortality as it is, we are not truly living. It is never too late not to waste any more of life, for it is a gift we are given to live, not to reason the how, why and wherefore as to our being here. Let's not waste another moment of this precious gift. Life is unfolding as it should. God has a purpose for you and me, and we must let go and allow Him to do His work, for all will unfold for our betterment in His good time.

There was one far greater than all the philosophers, teachers and seekers of enlightenment and truth. That one was Yeshua, a Hebrew name, in the Greek form Iēsous, which was later adopted and became the name Jesus in English and other languages. At his death on the cross, it was written as an abbreviation for the Latin phrase "Iesus Nazarenus Rex Iudaeorum," which translates to "Jesus of Nazareth, King of the Jews". This phrase was written above Jesus on the cross by Pontius Pilate. Jesus was born between 6 and 4 BC. He is believed to have died between 30 and 36 AD. Most scholars place his death around AD 30 or 33.

Although born in Bethlehem, according to the Gospels of Matthew and Luke, Jesus was a Galilean from Nazareth, a village near Sepphoris, one of the two major cities of Galilee. He was born to Joseph and Mary shortly before the death of Herod the Great (Matthew 2; Luke 1:5) in 4 BCE. According to Matthew and Luke, however, Joseph was only legally his father. They report that Mary was a virgin when Jesus was conceived and she "was found to be with child from the Holy Spirit" (Matthew 1:18; *cf.* Luke 1:35). Joseph is said to have been a carpenter (Matthew 13:55), and, according to Mark 6:3, Jesus also became a carpenter.

Luke (2:41-52) states that Jesus, as a youth, was precocious and learned, yet there is no additional evidence of his childhood or early life. It is reported that at the age of twelve, he entered the temple and began teaching the scribes and priests the true meaning of the scriptures, which they misunderstood. As a young adult, he was baptised by the prophet John the Baptist in the River Jordan. As soon as Jesus was baptised, he came out of the water. At that moment, heaven opened, and he saw the Spirit of God descending like a dove and resting on him. A voice from heaven then said, "This is my Son, whom I love; with him I am well pleased." Jesus was then led by the Spirit into the wilderness to be tempted by the devil. After fasting for forty days and nights, he was hungry. The tempter came to him and said, "If you are the Son of God, tell these stones to become bread." Jesus answered, "It is written: 'Man shall not live on bread alone, but on every word that comes from the mouth of God.'" Then the devil took him to the holy city and had him stand on the highest point of the temple. "If you are the

Son of God," he said, "throw yourself down. It is written: 'He will command his angels concerning you, and they will lift you in their hands, so that you will not strike your foot against a stone.'" Jesus replied, 'It is also written: 'Do not put the Lord your God to the test.'" Again, the devil took him to a very high mountain and showed him all the kingdoms of the world and their splendour. "All this I will give you," he said, "if you will bow down and worship me." Jesus replied, "Away from me, Satan! For it is written: 'Worship the Lord your God, and serve him only.'" Then the devil left him, and angels came and attended him.

Immediately after his time in the wilderness, Jesus became an itinerant preacher and healer (Mark 1:2 28). In his mid-30s, Jesus had a short public career, lasting perhaps less than one year, and he attracted considerable attention. Sometime between 29 and 33 CE —possibly 30 CE—he went to observe the Passover in Jerusalem, where his entrance, according to the Gospels, was triumphant and infused with spiritual significance. While there, he was arrested, tried, and executed. His disciples became convinced that he rose from the dead and appeared to them. They converted others to his belief, which eventually led to the formation of a new religion, Christianity.

Jesus was not widely known beyond the regions in which he travelled on earth. According to the New Testament, the principal locations for Jesus' ministry were Galilee and Judea, with activities also taking place in surrounding areas, such as Perea and Samaria. Socrates was well-known throughout his time, but Jesus was not. It was the work of Paul in preaching to all nations, the trust and power of Jesus through the Holy Spirit, that caught fire. To this day, unlike all the teachers and philosophers of ages past, the testament and power of Jesus' love remain. However, the Holy Spirit stands above all else and is everlasting.

CHAPTER 8.

MORE MYTHICAL STORIES

The Camino Frances, also known as the French Way, is steeped in mythical stories and legends. Many of these relate to the Apostle James the Greater, the miracles attributed to him, and the pilgrimage associated with him. These stories often intertwine with local folklore and historical events, creating a rich tapestry of tales that enhance the journey. The Camino de Santiago is the way to the tomb of St. James, spanning some 800 kilometres across northern Spain, following the Camino de Santiago, the 'field of Stars,' the Milky Way that has been mythically outlined by the apostle himself, leading to his final tomb underneath the altar at the Cathedral in Santiago.

In my three Camino Pilgrimages, I now recall real events and myths that motivated me to write novels, which fired up my imagination, all with The Way as the template to shape the stories that later unfolded. The first of my adventures was letting go of the many painful events that had engulfed my life over the previous decade. The broad journey of my Camino was more than a geographic excursion. The journey presented me with the many pilgrims I met along the Way who were either entering a new state of life. Like the young as a rite of passage, to those who were there to figure something out in a spirit of awareness, or those like me in recovery, or after living so long in the material world, were learning for the first time in their lives to let go of the baggage and walk with a sense of new freedom.

Once the elixir of the Way had entered the marrow of my bones, I could not help but return. The first journey sparked my imagination, and I returned to write a book of poems, a novel, and record an album of songs. All of which I had no idea would happen to me. I returned to a new route on the Camino, this time in search of love, but all I found in the pursuit of sexual pleasure was disappointment and hard lessons in the substitution of lust for love. If nothing else, the lotus flower of creative ideas continued, and another novel and a second album of songs followed.

Soon enough, I was back on the French route again, this time having learnt the lessons of letting go, letting God, and not chasing the myths so much as just letting things unfold. I had slipped back into a state of depression for a time before I ventured back on The Way again, but I was determined to be led wherever the road less travelled would take me. Not only did I recover from my mental issues, but I also found the power of contemplation and creative outpouring multiplied into even more books and songs. It is now that eight years have elapsed since my last Camino journey, and I look back with an even greater awakening of the spirit within.

My conscious self has become more efficacious in living in the present. It may be because I have just passed the milestone of becoming an octogenarian, and wisdom is finally coming with age. Looking back on my Camino adventures and the previous decades, my experiences and story are somewhat mythical. Every moment now seems more precious than before, for I may not pass this way again. Thus, I will share some of the long-standing myths of The Way with you, dear reader, as many of the ancient myths and legends of the Camino de Santiago, particularly along the French route, are still believed today. The in-depth nature of these myths can be explored by checking them out on caminoway.com.au for a synopsis of my books.

It is from the foothill of the Pyrenees mountains that the climb on The Way begins, and the first marker of the Camino is passed. The entire 800 km pilgrimage to Santiago de Compostela features milestone guideposts along The Way, each marked by a scallop shell that denotes the various paths to Santiago. And where there is no marker, a yellow arrow points the way. The seashell symbol is steeped in mystery and symbolism. The yellow area has an honest and real significance, but here we are about myth.

The scallop shell is a metaphor for pilgrimage, representing the idea that the journey is more important than the destination. The Concha of Santiago can be traced back to when the disciple visited the Spanish peninsula by boat to bury the remains of St. James. Unfortunately, a storm destroyed the ship. After some time, St James's body was found undamaged and covered in scallop shells along the seashore. On their arrival at the Galician coast, the disciples saw a wedding on the shore. The bride was on horseback. Suddenly, the frightened horse dove into the ocean with the bride still in the saddle. Thankfully, the bride and the horse emerged from the water safe and sound, covered in scallop shells.

Another version associates the scallop shell with Venus, the goddess of love and beauty. Venus's symbol signifies the rebirth of people, symbolising the resurrection. Symbolic means overcoming the ego to move forward toward an authentic self, one that is more humble and simple. It also means beginnings and endings, transition and transformation—all ideas shared by pilgrims and discovered on the Camino today, a constant source of renewal and rediscovery. [In my song Santiago Traveller, with album of the same name, further insight into the seashell can be listened to - YouTube Top songs Doug McPhillips]

The climb of the Pyrenees after leaving St. Jean Pied de Port starts on the French side of the route into Spain. The pilgrim may recall that this is the route of the famous Frankish General Charlemagne, who fought many battles throughout Europe as a conquering hero and later became the King of France. Charlemagne first crossed the Pyrenees to campaign against the Moors in 778. This campaign involved invading northern Spain, which was then controlled by the Moors, and included the capture of Pamplona. However, the expedition ended with a significant defeat at the Battle of Roncevaux Pass on the return journey, a notable event immortalised in the epic poem The Song of Roland.

The Legend of Roland, particularly as recounted in the "Song of Roland," is a pivotal aspect of medieval literature and culture. It features Roland, a Frankish hero and Charlemagne's nephew, who faces a fateful encounter in the Pyrenees mountains. While drawing on historical events, the legend also blends historical fact and fantastical elements, portraying Roland as a brave and loyal warrior. The story is rooted in the historical Battle of Roncesvalles in 778, where Basque forces ambushed a Frankish rear guard led by Roland. It is not only the story of Roland as hero of the battle to the death with the giant of the Moor's army, but also the mythology of his wielding of his sword 'Durandal'. The French Excalibur, a legendary sword, was once wielded by the young Charlemagne in his numerous battles throughout Europe and Britain. It was given as a gift to Roland by his uncle Charlemagne when he appointed Roland the head of the rear guard of his army. Durandal, it is said, contained within its golden hilt a tooth of Saint Peter, blood of Basil of Caesarea, hair of Saint Denis, and a piece of the raiment of Mary, the mother of Jesus. The sword is famous for its hardness and sharpness.

In Roland's story, his real guard is ambushed by Bargue warriors under the instruction of the Moors. As Charlemagne's main army contingent had taken the mountainous route back to France, Roland was left to ensure that no Moorish forces were along the lower valley way. Unfortunately, the enemy lay hidden in a narrow gorge, trapping the retreating army.

Legend has it that Roland fought to the death against a Saracen giant, Ferragut, whom he had previously encountered in the Moors' defence of the city of Nájera against Roland and his forces. Roland and Ferragut engage once more in a fierce battle, and in some tales, Roland's success against the giant is depicted as a David and Goliath scenario. He killed the giant at his weakest point by plunging the Durandal sword into the giant's navel. Roland blows his 'Oliphant' elephant tusk horn in a last-ditch call for help when hopelessly outnumbered. In the action, he burst his temples and, before dying, hurled the blade so hard that it flew for over 100 miles before piercing a rock 32 feet above the ground. In another version, he embeds the sword in a crevice in a nearby rock, where it remains, never to be removed. This version may also be linked to the story of King Arthur's Excalibur, the legendary sword of King Arthur, which was given to him by the Lady of the Lake. It's often associated with Arthur's right to rule and is known for its magical properties. While some tales portray

Excalibur as belonging solely to Arthur, others suggest his knights also wielded it. The King Arthur mythological story originated in a tale written by Geoffrey of Monmouth in the 12th century.

There was a final account of Charlemagne returning to find the dead Roland with the sword hidden under his body, and later using it in many more battles in defence against Moorish troops. In the Song of Roland, the account of this tale is the first poem ever written in French literature. So the legend lives on, like the prophecy of Charlemagne tells of the sword from stone. Like the legend of King Arthur, the prophecy of pulling Excalibur from a stone adds more to the myth than a real event.

As the pilgrim traverses the mountainous regions of the Pyrenees and journeys to the next stage of the Camino, almost 13 km from Pamplona, the intrepid traveller will find the Reniega Fountain, the enclave of one of the most famous myths on the Camino de Santiago. According to this tale of pilgrim culture, a pilgrim was completing a challenging climb in the middle of summer on the Pass of Perdon. Upon reaching the pass, thirsty and exhausted, he found only dirt and dust. At that moment, the devil appeared disguised as a young pilgrim walker, and the thirsty pilgrim asked him where he could get some water. The demon quickly offered the dying pilgrim to soothe his thirst if he rejected God. According to the legend of the Reniega Fountain, the pilgrim refused to renounce his faith in God. It was then that the devil tried to tempt him again, asking him to surrender the Virgin Mary if he wanted to quench his thirst. The dying pilgrim refused his offer again. Satan, convinced that he would make the pilgrim renounce his faith, made him a third offer. *"If you forget your devotion to Santiago the Apostle, I will soothe your thirst and you'll avoid death,"* the devil told him. Despite the desire to drink some water, the pilgrim said no again. The thirsty man, looking exhausted and weak, and at the high price demanded by the devil for providing water, implored heaven for help. The legend has it that the Reniega Fountain tells that at that moment, the devil disappeared, wrapped in a cloud of sulphur. In the eyes of the surprised pilgrim, Santiago appeared as a pilgrim. The apostle made a fountain appear, in the same place, from which fresh and clean water emanated. With it, he gave some for the pilgrim to drink, using his scallop. The myth has shades of the story of Jesus being tempted by the devil in the wilderness, as well as the miracles associated with devotion to the Virgin Mary. According to the peasants of this region, the fountain's water saved many pilgrims who came to her seriously ill. They also say that the Virgin of Forgiveness works miracles among the neighbours of this area of the Camino de Santiago.

Another Virgin Mary story unfolds on the long plains before Santo Domingo in the village of Estella. In the early history of the Camino, shepherds gathered on the hillsides to defend themselves from wild animals and bandits. One night, in the area where the town of Estella now stands, they noticed an unusual number of shooting stars falling from the peak of the mountain that towers over the valley; they decided to climb up to see what was happening. Once they arrived, they discovered a statue of the Virgin Mary inside a cave. Surprised by this extraordinary find, they tried to transport the statue to the local church for safekeeping. Despite the combined efforts of the shepherds, the statue remained still. The people from the valley, well impressed by this miracle, decided to build a sanctuary around the statue, and they called the city which rose around it "Estella". If a strange force was keeping it in place, the people from the valley, well impressed by this miracle, decided to build a sanctuary around the statue. They called the city that rose around it Estella, meaning star.

Legend has it that a particular pilgrim from Lapurdi, in the French Basque Country, roamed the treacherous lands of the northern Pyrenees peninsula near Roncesvalles. If these lands were harmful, it was due to the many bandits and robbers that had roamed these roads, attacking pilgrims on the road to Santiago de Compostela. Just one of these pilgrims decided to spend the night at an inn in this mountainous area to shelter from the dark. When he was already in his room, he was surprised by another pilgrim, apparently also seeking shelter.

In the spirit of Camino charity, he opened his bedroom to the stranger. He offered to walk the route together to Santiago de Compostela to ward off the calamities that might be encountered. The new host agreed to accompany him, and both continued the next morning. Still, little did the idyllic alliance know that when both pilgrims penetrated a remote wooded area of all prying eyes, our pilgrim turned his back to be treacherously stabbed. His new companion was a crooked man who had chosen a strategy to deceive the pilgrim, earning his trust.

The miseries of our pilgrim multiplied when the villain found, upon searching, that he had nothing of actual value in his possession, so that stripping him of all their belongings and throwing him down a hillside as God brought the end to his world, he lay there bleeding to death. Unable to prevent the night enveloping him, the pilgrim, unable to move, checked his fate, and saw a herd of wolves directly approaching him. Despite his sorry state, the pilgrim could see a glow emanating from the eyes of one of the wolves, which confirmed that he was just a few feet away.

Thus, our pilgrim could die in peace and face eternal rest; he prayed for St. James of Santiago to come for the salvation of his soul, knowing that his sad end was near. Legend has it that the wolf's luminous eyes spooked the herd, causing them to stop in their tracks. Hence, the pilgrim lived long enough before his final rest in peace, and Santiago faced an important charge: ultimately, to avenge the unfortunate pilgrim.

His executioner, the twisted villain, continued his walk along the pilgrimage route until he decided to stop at a mountain hut, thinking he was safe. Still, in the middle of the night, when his snoring was at its deepest, he was surprised by a pack of wolves, led by an owl with luminous eyes, behind the legend who was the Apostle Santiago. Despite his awkward stabs at the air with his still-stained knife, the villain was slain by the wolves, overseen at all times by the mysterious protective figure, who never would have taken sides, keeping score.

A soul legend of Santiago, embodied as a wolf, aligns with the belief that wolves are said to remember the day of their death. Every hundred years, pilgrims have heard the wolf's howl echoing all night, compelling thugs to pause outside his office for a day should they wish to meet the wolf's luminous eyes. Centuries later, this wolf transformed into a legendary figure who protected pilgrims every hundred years as they crossed the Pyrenees.

However, we worry that today, the real threats are not the villains we fear the most in this mountainous destination.

The legend of the rooster in the church is yet another popular soul legend of Santiago. It centres around a German pilgrim, Hugonell, who was falsely accused of theft while on the Camino. He was sentenced to be hanged, but his parents heard his voice, claiming that Saint Dominic had saved him. The parents rushed to the local mayor, who was having dinner, and scoffed at the claim, stating that their son was no more alive than the rooster and hen he was about to eat. As he said this, the birds leapt off the plate, sprouted feathers, and began to crow.

This event is commemorated at the Cathedral of Santo Domingo de la Calzada, where live roosters and hens are kept in a henhouse throughout the year. The birds are always white and donated by devotees of the saint, who bring new pairs each month. Finding a feather from one of these birds is believed to bring good luck to the pilgrim, and some think that hearing the rooster crow while in the church is a sign of favour from St. Dominic.

Another well-known story of the Camino de Santiago unfolds in the heart of Santiago de Compostela, adjacent to the Cathedral. It is known as the legend of the Shadow of the Pilgrim and the Legend of the Ghost Pilgrim.

This pilgrim tale speaks of love, the romance between a priest and a cloistered nun. This story of the Camino de Santiago takes place in the Plaza de la Quintana, one of the most visited squares in Santiago de Compostela after the Plaza del Obradoiro. The most widespread version of this story tells us that a priest in the cathedral once fell in love with a cloistered nun from the nearby Convent of San Paio. The lovers met through an underground passageway that connected the two temples. Tired of that clandestine situation, the clergyman proposed to his beloved that they flee together and start a new life. The lovers met at nightfall in the Plaza de la Quintana. He had arranged to meet his lover in the square, but she never arrived. It is said that he is still waiting for her there. At sunset, his shadow appears on a wall of the Cathedral.

There is the case of the pilgrim's shadow, which is produced by the lamp that illuminates the corner of Santiago Cathedral where the façades of the Royal Gate and the ambulatory converge. The light is projected onto the walls, creating the stage and the stone landmark that covers the lightning rod of the immense clock tower. The result is the static figure of a pilgrim on the pedestal of one of the columns flanking the Royal Gate. The origin of the pilgrim's shadow is therefore clearly visible. There is nothing special about it, beyond its perfectly recognisable shape: the silhouette of a pilgrim with his staff. Yet, it has been linked to a much older legend, which tells of several crimes, a prisoner, a punishment, and a curse.

The most famous Camino myth is associated with the Battle of Clavijo. Saint James miraculously appeared to assist an outnumbered Spanish Christian army, helping them gain a victory against the Moors, who had begun their conquest of Hispania in AD 711. According to legend, Saint James appeared as a warrior on a white horse amidst the Spanish army, wielding a fiery sword. Upon seeing him, the Christian military cried, "¡Dios ayuda a Santiago!"-"God save St. James!" It is believed that more than 5,000 Moors were killed during the battle, earning James the title "Moor-slayer". Many historians argue that the Battle of Clavijo never occurred and that it is a myth. The legend only appeared in writing nearly 300 years after its alleged occurrence. St James, "one of the strongest ideological icons", has helped establish its national identity.

Some people believe that the Camino to Santiago existed long before Christianity transformed it into what it is now: a route you follow to eventually reach the cathedral, where you can visit the remains of a saint. Some people believe that the route, following the way of the stars, was already there when people believed in multiple gods, usually related to nature and its phenomena. Those cultures created monuments in specific locations with a certain energy or cosmic alignment. A route of lay lines and water veins for souls to follow until the end of the world, Finisterre. Whatever you believe, the Celtic roots left a permanent magical veil around Galicia, and you can see and feel it while roaming the Galician highlands.

CHAPTER 9.

THE LAST HURRAH

We often inadvertently use the phrase "as sure as death." Come to think of it, its true meaning — it represents certainty. There is nothing more certain, as the end is a one-hundred-per-cent certainty amidst the entire unpredictability of the universe. Despite having this knowledge, it isn't easy to grasp this phenomenon. In almost all cultures around the world, people avoid discussing death; in fact, joking about it is frowned upon. It is as if a reference to this word itself is viewed as inauspicious.

If there is life, death is inevitable. Not discussing this allows us to deny its existence, and thus, effectively pushes it to the unused shelves of our subconscious, to be dealt with only when the event occurs in reality. The ways of death are mysterious. We often plan our everyday life for the next day, month, year, and life events. We are unaware of death's schemes. Sometimes he is polite enough to knock and provide a warning, at other times, he loves to spring a surprise. More often than not, he comes like a thief in the night. Death comes to us all, regardless of our skills, efforts, aspirations, and actions.

In my lifetime, I've witnessed death on numerous occasions, some blood relatives who died suddenly and what seemed unfair before they had reached their full potential. Others who seem to have it all and yet took their own life through not being able to cope any more with living, or had forgotten about the fact of the need to suffer to understand how to live and conquer fear or the demons that come to possess us all from time to time.

Some say we die when we complete the purpose for which we are born. Each of us is unique, and we all have a distinct impact on our surroundings. We may not realise it in the day-to-day affairs of things, but we make the world better every day by following our passion and doing our best. What then is that seemingly normal moment that makes us extraordinary and defines the precise time we fulfil our purpose? Is our existence made meaningful before death comes knocking? Those exact moments are difficult to pinpoint.

Each moment I exist in is essential. I have no control over death. No control over the manner or the time at which he will choose to come. Hence, the best course is to live in every moment and give my all to my life and the lives around me, so that today makes perfect sense, as if there is no tomorrow. When tomorrow comes, make it just as meaningful as today. So that when my time comes, I can go on into the unknown and be happy that I loved my time on earth. And all these people I lost, loved, or indeed made amends to along the way, they too have that epiphany at some point.

So, whatever our skills, aspirations, and actions in life, the grim reaper comes to meet us all. Whether strong or weak, clever or ignorant, rich or poor, good or evil, we must all eventually bow to the great leveller. Death is the only absolute certainty in life [tax seems to be another certainty]. Death remains the greatest of all enigmas, for no matter how scientifically sophisticated we become, we cannot solve the mystery of what happens to us when we die. Humans have long believed that something survives beyond the physical shell that decays and returns to dust. Myths have been expressed in imaginative forms of human fears, fantasies, and expectations of death. Religions have always attempted to offer certainties about the life hereafter, teaching us that our adherence to a particular dogma during life guarantees us an alternative; metaphors and images which ultimately guarantee nothing, but somehow communicate meaning and value to death. Myths lend meaning and value to death, making it a part of life and a necessary chapter in the grand cosmic cycle. Nothing we may study or seek offers answers to this great mystery as to death, and indeed, why we live at all.

So when this corruptible has put on incorruption, and this mortal has put on immortality, the written saying shall be brought to pass: "Death is swallowed up in victory." "O Death, where is your sting? O Hades, where is your victory?" (1 Corinthians 15:51)

Those who believe in God, particularly Jesus, death and resurrection, have some connection with the mystery of the afterlife and seem to fear less than most facing life after death, in the belief of being saved to enter the heavenly kingdom.

The Apostle Paul reserved the greatest blessing of the Resurrection for his final point. He likened death to a bee which had lost its stinger and then taunted it by asking, "O Death, where is your sting? O Hades, where is your victory?" Just as the grave could not hold Jesus, it will be incapable of holding Christians. We already have victory over death "through our Lord Jesus Christ"

Why should we fear death when we understand our glorious future with Christ? The power of death has been conquered.

Perhaps it is why many Christian martyrs have given their lives to share the gospel. These brave men and women did not fear losing what they could not keep to gain what they could not lose. The worst thing the world can do to us is to kill us; yet, ironically, that is the best thing that can happen to us.

So, how should we respond to this amazing truth? Paul concluded the "Resurrection chapter" by stating, "Therefore, my beloved brethren, be steadfast, immovable, always abounding in the work of the Lord, knowing that your labour is not in vain in the Lord" (1 Corinthians 15:58). Don't spend your life chasing earthly pleasures. Instead, live each moment of every day for Christ, because the Resurrection guarantees that our work done for the Lord is not wasted.

If one dares to follow nature's instinct, character defects may lead one to fall into the abyss of pleasurable acts in a world of ultimate sorrow, shame, and pain. In contrast, we must balance our better nature by embracing the spiritual way to the light without being blinded by the good that comes from it in the form of love.

Living in the balance between the physical and spiritual world isn't easy, and there comes a time when we might want to check our hearts. Perhaps the reason we turn to others and things is a matter of love and treasure. Maybe we've slowly let them have more affection than they are worth. Rather than a complete satisfaction in the physical with a mild interest in the spiritual, we want total satisfaction in our Saviour with a light hold on this world.

So those of us who believe in a higher power have hope, not the fear of an afterlife. As we age, we tend to look back more on our lives, as looking forward, there is less time to live. So, the hope of tomorrow to finish what we have started or to pray for a peaceful death seems all we can do.

Nature appears to be the best source of understanding that death is not an end, but a crucial part of the life cycle. It facilitates the recycling of resources, drives evolution, and creates space for new growth and competition. Organisms that die provide nutrients for the soil and the environment, supporting the development of new life. Additionally, death plays a vital role in natural selection, where less-adapted individuals are eliminated, allowing better-adapted individuals to thrive and pass on their genes, thereby shaping the course of evolution.

It is when looking back that we find reasons to regret rather than treasure those things that led to good will for others. The St. Francis of Assisi prayer was for him a daily mission statement of action-centred focus, emphasising what he could do for others rather than himself, with a mindset of acting with a positive outlook —a glass-half-full approach to life. Staying in the present is the best way to live, taking one day at a time - the only way to reach any longer-term objective. Enjoy each day as it comes, every moment as if it will be the last. For one day, it will be so. On a time basis, I am confident that I can live freely, knowing I will be the best version of myself. So I set out with confidence. Then, I will receive a reward for my achievement. Knowing this at the end of the day makes me feel good and motivates me to strive for more.

The belief in God is the central message of Ecclesiastes in the bible. It is the inherent meaninglessness of life's pursuits without God, a concept often summarised as "hevel" or "vanity". The author explores the futility of seeking happiness through worldly achievements, pleasures, and even wisdom, as these ultimately lead to a sense of emptiness. Instead, the book encourages a life of reverent worship and obedience to God, recognising that true meaning and hope are found in the hope of God's future judgment and justice. It seems that only by handing over to God and being mindful of using our talents for the benefit of others does our life become richer, and we may find true happiness, an extra dividend of giving to others without any demand in return. Then our focus is not on our end, but on enjoying life as it may be presented to us daily.

Then there's the link between death and love. Love, especially in its most profound forms, is often intertwined with the concept of death in various ways. One perspective suggests that love involves a willingness to die for one's beloved. Another idea is that love can be a form of "dying to oneself" to embrace and nurture another person. Additionally, love is viewed as a connection to mortality, reminding us of our finite existence. The quote "Greater love hath no man than this, that a man lay down his life for his friends" is from the Bible, specifically John 15:13. It means that the ultimate expression of love is to sacrifice oneself for others. In essence, it highlights the idea that true love entails prioritising the needs and well-being of others above one's own, even to the point of self-sacrifice, if necessary.

Through reflection, mindfulness, spirituality, and support when facing the fear of death, we can find the strength to embrace death as a natural part of life. By living with purpose, practising gratitude, educating ourselves, and engaging in meaningful conversations, we can develop a profound acceptance of our finite existence. Whatever our timely end, death is not something we want to focus on too much, but at some point in time, the bridge from life to death must be crossed.

The lyrics to Harry Manx's "Don't You Forget to Miss Me" seem to sum it all up.

What is this that I can't see
Cold mist is running all over me
Stretch my eyes, wanna stretch my limbs
Ain't that the way that death begins

Oh well
Old death, have mercy, death be easy now
Oh, pass me over now for another year
Another year

You were the flower of my death, come
Cut you down oh so soon
You were the flower of my death, come
Cut you down oh so soon

Old death, have mercy, death be easy now
Oh, pass me over now for another year
Another year
Another year

Old death, death be easy now, death be easy
Old death, pass me over now
Another year
Another year

Only then will your house be blessed
So, don't forget to miss me.
                    - Harry Manx.

What is this life if full of care,
We have no time to stand and stare.

No time to stand beneath the boughs
And stare as long as sheep or cows.

No time to see when we pass the woods,
Where squirrels hide their nuts in the grass.

No time to see, in broad daylight,
Streams full of stars, like skies at night.

No time to turn at Beauty's glance,
And watch her feet, how they can dance.

No time to wait till her mouth can
Enrich that smile, her eyes began.

A poor life this, full of care,
We have no time to stand and stare.

CHAPTER 10.

EPILOGUE

The biblical definition of duplicity states: "A double-minded man is unstable in all his ways (James 1:8). When one is crafty, it is either to give one or two impressions to mislead an individual, only for the trickster's benefit. Either impression may be false, or both may be false. It's a crafty game built on deception. Equally, if one were to stand between light and dark, I would say it would be to take a neutral position, so such a state is not living either in the world nor in the spirit, but being an avoidant. We must take a stand, one step at a time, and therein lies progress. We must walk the tightrope carefully, avoiding duplicity and the avoidance of intimacy or social contact, but being consciously aware of defining and examining the dark.

I'd hand the guidance on this dilemma over to those of greater faith than I possess. It seems only reasonable to me that such teachings are best described in biblical teachings, rather than those of philosophers, mythical fables, or symbols and signs that may appear to answer but are often disguised by my egocentric guidelines and those of intellect, rather than the spiritual utterance of good intent. The concept of being "in the world but not of the world" is a central theme in Christian theology, as expressed in various passages throughout the Bible. These passages emphasise the need for believers to live in the world, engage with it, and witness it, while maintaining a distinct identity and not being absorbed by its values and systems.

Here are some key scriptures that address this concept:

Jesus prays for his disciples, saying, "I have given them your word, and the world has hated them, because they are not of the world, even as I am not. I do not ask that you take them out of the world, but keep them from the evil one. They are not of the world, even as I am not of the world." This passage highlights the separation of believers from the world, yet also emphasises their need to remain in the world to be witnesses for Christ. John 17:14-16:. Then, another passage from John (2:15-17) warns believers against loving the world, even for material gain, the pleasures of the flesh, or power. He emphasises, "Whoever loves the world, the love of the Father is not in him." It encourages a focus on God's love and a rejection of worldly attachments.

In his writings to the Corinthians (1 Corinthians 5:20), Paul describes Christians as "ambassadors for Christ," urging them to reconcile with God. This verse suggests that while believers are in the world, they have a specific role in representing Christ and his kingdom to others. He reminds Christians in Philippians 3:20 that their citizenship is in heaven, emphasising their higher calling and encouraging them to focus on the things of heaven rather than the things of the world.

These scriptures, and others like them, convey that Christians are called to live in the world as a distinct community, reflecting Christ's values and principles while engaging with the world to share the message of salvation. They are not to withdraw from the world but are to remain in it, living as ambassadors for Christ and shining as lights in a dark world.

Paul had no illusions about the dark side of his nature or how often he fell to its forces, but he equally trusted in the power of

God and Jesus' influence in following the path of righteousness. Paul wrote in Romans 7:15-20 about his struggles between the dark side of his nature and the spirit of the path he trod in the love of God through his preaching. "What I do not understand is what I do. For what I want to do, I do not do, but what I hate, I do. [16] I agree that the law is good if I do what I do not want to do. [17] As it is, I no longer do it, but sin is living in me. [18] For I know that good itself does not dwell in me, that is, in my sinful nature.[a] For I desire to do what is good, but I cannot carry it out. [19] For I do not do the good I want to do, but the evil I do not want to do—this I keep on doing. [20] Now, if I do what I do not want to, it is no longer me who does it; it is sin living in me who does it."

In Corinthians 23:48, Paul states, " Love is patient and kind; love does not envy or boast; it is not arrogant or rude. It does not insist on its way; it is not irritable or resentful; it does not rejoice at wrongdoing, but rejoices with the truth. St. Paul's writings emphasise that love is the most important thing. He states that if he could speak in any language, even divine ones, if he had the gift of prophecy, or faith that could move mountains, but lacked love, he would be nothing. He also says that if he gave everything away or even sacrificed his body, but did not have love, he would gain nothing. In other words, St. Paul highlights that all abilities and accomplishments are meaningless without love. Love is not just a feeling; it's a powerful force that motivates actions and interactions with others. In 1 Corinthians 13, Paul describes love as patient, kind, not jealous, and enduring all things. He stresses that love never fails and is the best way to live.

This emphasis on love is a recurring theme in St. Paul's writings, particularly in his letters to the Corinthians. He uses the concept of love to address division, conflict, and the misuse of spiritual gifts within the church. By prioritising love, Paul encourages believers to act with humility, compassion, and a focus on the well-being of others.

The content of this book will be taken in good faith, for it has been an adventure in recalling lightbulb moments along the way and rekindling my spirit of miracles upon awakening. Likewise, I hope with a sincere heart that it benefits our inward movement toward the spirit and serves as a roadmap to enhance the pathway for what remains of this journey that you and I are embarking upon, until death do us part.

About the Author

Doug McPhillips, a poet, singer, songwriter, and author, began his journey of discovery more than a decade ago, following a series of life-changing events.

The many paths he has traversed throughout the Northern Hemisphere and down under in New Zealand and Australia have shaped the facts and fiction of this novel.

Doug has written twenty-one novels, two poetry books, a travel guide, and three albums of his songs, all inspired by his adventures.

www.ingramcontent.com/pod-product-compliance
Lightning Source LLC
Chambersburg PA
CBHW052207090526
44583CB00017BA/2411